BEFORE THE FOUNDATION OF THE WORLD

DOCTRINES OF GOD'S FREE GRACE

A Confessional Perspective

BEFORE THE FOUNDATION OF THE WORLD

DOCTRINES OF GOD'S FREE GRACE

A Confessional Perspective

Jeffrey T. Riddle

Broken Wharfe

BEFORE THE FOUNDATION OF THE WORLD

DOCTRINES OF GOD'S FREE GRACE

A Confessional Perspective

First published as *The Doctrines of Grace: An Introduction to the Five Points of Calvinism* by Trumpet Books in 2019.

Unless otherwise noted, all scripture quotations are from The Authorized (King James) Version, public domain (US).

ISBN 978-1-7393653-4-9

Broken Wharfe

This book was edited by Broken Wharfe.

Typeset in Adobe Garamond Pro by Jill Sawyer Phypers
Printed in the UK by TJ Books Ltd, Padstow, Cornwall
Cover art: © Jude May Design
www.judemaydesign.com
Cover images © SweetGrace | iStock

brokenwharfe.com

In *Before the Foundation of the World*, pastor Riddle synopsizes Biblical doctrines that have all too frequently been overlooked. It is very important for Christians and those who desire to be Christians to understand these doctrines, as they have to do with salvation itself. How does the sovereign God of the Bible bring us into a saving relationship with himself through Jesus Christ? This book deals with this matter in a manner that can be readily understood by the reader. I heartily commend it.

W. GARY CRAMPTON
Research Professor of Theology, Whitefield Theological Seminary, Lakeland, FL

With the renewed interest in the Doctrines of Grace around the world in recent years, Jeff Riddle has put us in his debt by producing this up-to-date and modest, yet comprehensive, exposition on the subject. He points out that the doctrine (singular) of God's grace in salvation is composed of several foundational and inter-related doctrines (plural). The introduction of the book sketches the history of the formulation of these doctrines and the central place it occupies in Reformed and biblical theology, summarised under the acronym TULIP. Each of the 'five points' is expounded in the subsequent chapters by showing its scriptural basis and meaning, followed by answers to common objections, and the conclusion of the matter. This book will be helpful to those who are new to the Doctrines of Grace, and a helpful resource for teaching the biblical doctrine of salvation in the mid-week Bible Study in church, in a church camp, and among Christian students in the campus.

BOON-SING POH
Pastor, Damansara Reformed Baptist Church (DRBC), Kuala Lumpur, Malaysia

Like all the best books on theology, Jeff Riddle's little book on the doctrines of grace started life as teaching for Dr Riddle's church. This book comes from the pen of a pastor who is committed to the growth of his congregation in their love for the gospel and their depth of wisdom and insight—it is accessible and heart-warming theology as its best.

As well as offering a very clear exposition of each of the five points of Calvinism—showing the biblical basis for each point and touching on historical discussions where helpful—Dr Riddle also provides an accessible defence of systematic theology and confessionalism, as well as an explanation of the term "Reformed". This is one of the best introductions to the doctrines of grace and how to think theologically, that I know of. If you are looking for a book to introduce the uninitiated to the doctrines of grace, this is the book.

JONATHAN WOODROW
Pastor of Christ Church, Loughborough, UK

For the members of Christ Reformed Baptist Church of Louisa, Virginia

Contents

Preface

I have sometimes been asked when it was that I became a Calvinist. I cannot give a certain answer to this question. I like to think that I became a Calvinist before I ever knew anything about John Calvin or Reformed theology. I was raised in a family and in small rural churches in South Carolina and North Carolina where the Scriptures were received as the Word of God. As a young Christian I was a Biblicist. It was from reading the Bible and hearing it taught and preached that I concluded God is sovereign over all things, including salvation.

Many years later when I graduated from seminary in Louisville, Kentucky, a local church handed out reprint copies of James P. Boyce's Abstract of Systematic Theology, and as a bibliophile I, of course, picked up a copy. That volume stayed in a box in the attic of my in-laws for two years while my wife and I served as short term missionaries in Budapest, Hungary. When we got home and I began to serve as a pastor in my first church, I read that volume and was heartened to discover that much systematic thought had been given to what I was beginning to understand as the doctrines of grace. I was set on a path to become not only a Calvinist but a confessional Reformed Baptist.

The content of this book represents some of my efforts to teach others about these doctrines, which I have found to be so soul-satisfying. It began as a series of articles in the Evangelical Forum Newsletter. Then, it was used in a sermon series on the doctrine of salvation. It became a PDF that I would share with those who came to my church, who had also, by God's providence, stumbled upon these doctrines and were eager to learn more about them. My prayer is that this work will prove profitable for those who read it in this revised presentation.

This work aims to be simple and direct in its presentation of these doctrines, keeping close to Scriptural instruction. It is not exhaustive and makes no claim to infallibility. I have profited from receiving the instruction and encouragement of many who may not always be cited directly within these pages. My thanks to my wife Llewellyn and my children for their constant support. My thanks also to Dr. W. Gary Crampton of Richmond, Virginia and Dr. Boon-Sing Poh of Kuala Lampur, Malaysia who read drafts of this manuscript and offered helpful feedback. Thanks also to Debbie Florentine, a member of Christ Reformed Baptist Church, for her help in editing and formatting this work for publication. Any errors within it remain my own.

Soli Deo Gloria!

Jeffrey T. Riddle,
Pastor, Christ Reformed Baptist Church
Louisa, Virginia

Introduction
THE DOCTRINES
OF GRACE

Christians have heartily sung or recited the text of Newton's classic hymn, "Amazing Grace." We use the word "Grace" to name our Christian churches and schools.[1] We have even named our daughters "Grace." Christians are indeed familiar with the biblical word "grace" (Greek: *charis*). We generally know its simple definition as God's "unmerited favour" extended in the salvation of sinners. We readily recall the apostle Paul's foundational use of the term in Ephesians 2:8–9 when he writes, "For by grace are ye saved through faith; and that not of yourselves: it is the gift of God: Not of works, lest any man should boast." Still, we must consider whether we have truly grasped the profound nature of the biblical teaching of God's grace in salvation. Could it be that the term has been so often used that its understanding has become dulled?

This study aims to examine afresh the biblical doctrine of God's grace in salvation. In so doing, we recognize that the doctrine (singular) of God's grace in salvation is composed of several foundational and interrelated doctrines (plural). This plural term, "the doctrines of

---

[1] A friend of mine once observed that he knew of many "Grace Baptist Churches," "Grace Community Churches," and "Grace Christian Schools," but he had never yet seen a "Law Baptist Church" or a "Law Christian School," despite the fact that the Apostle Paul said, "Wherefore the law is holy, and the commandment holy, and just, and good" (Rom. 7:12), and "the law is good, if a man use it lawfully" (1 Tim. 1:8).

grace," has been used, therefore, to describe the systematic attempt to explain and describe the biblical teaching about God's free grace toward sinners in salvation. These essential doctrines include the need for grace (sin), the plan for grace (election), the means of grace (the cross), the attraction of grace (call), and the confidence of grace (assurance).

In this introduction we will provide an overview of some of the names and titles used in reference to the doctrines of grace and then offer a brief explanation of these doctrines as a theological system. Next, we will sketch a short history of the rise, fall, and revival of these doctrines. Finally, we will offer a brief summary and conclusion.

Reformed Theology and Calvinism

The doctrines of grace are generally associated with what is known as "Reformed Theology." This refers to the fact that these doctrines reflect biblical ideas about salvation reclaimed and espoused during the Protestant Reformation, a spiritual renewal movement which began in the sixteenth century and continues to this present day. The start of the Protestant Reformation is usually traced to October 31, 1517, when Martin Luther nailed his *Ninety-Five Theses* to the church door in Wittenberg, Germany, outlining his critiques of the medieval Roman Catholic church. For Luther the doctrine of salvation was a central focus in this critique, since he accused the Roman Church of neglecting and abandoning the biblical doctrine of justification by faith. Soon the Reformation spirit spread throughout Europe and beyond.

The doctrines of grace are also often referred to as "Calvinism" (or "the five points of Calvinism"), because they were promoted by the followers of John Calvin (1509–1564), the great Protestant Reformer of Geneva, Switzerland. Calvin is sometimes referred to as the "the Father of Reformed theology." Calvin was a prolific writer, teacher, and preacher. His most famous work was his *Institutes of the Christian Religion* (1536-1559). He also published commentaries on most of the books of the Bible. In his writings he did not explicitly group together and articulate "the five points" we now know as "the doctrines of grace." This would be done by his later intellectual and spiritual disciples and heirs. Some have even argued that Calvin did not in his own day affirm the doctrines of grace as they would be later articulated by his "Calvinistic" followers.[2] We can safely conclude, however, that Calvin's thought, as expressed in his writings, is in firm agreement with the doctrines of grace and that Calvin would have readily affirmed their necessary and logical relationship to each other.[3] Thus we can say that Calvin was a Calvinist!

A related question might be raised concerning the use of the term "Calvinistic." John Calvin's theology included many facets beyond the subject of soteriology (the doctrine of salvation). Calvin is also considered the father of Presbyterianism. He upheld infant baptism and the Presbyterian view of church government. In general, however, the term "Calvinist" or "Calvinistic", refers, in particular, to Calvin's doctrine of salvation. Thus, one does not have to be a Presbyterian or hold to infant baptism to be a "Calvinist".

We might then ask whether it is proper for a person to say that he is "Reformed" in theology simply because he holds to the doctrines of grace. The doctrines of grace, in fact, refer to only one aspect of Reformed theology, namely, the doctrine of salvation (soteriology). Full-orbed Reformed theology, however, includes other important distinctives: subscribing to a Reformed confession of faith, holding

---

[2] This argument is made by R. T. Kendall, *Calvin and English Calvinism to 1649* (Oxford: Oxford University Press, 1981).

[3] For a refutation of Kendall and an affirmation that the doctrines of grace do, indeed, rightly reflect the theology of John Calvin, see Paul Helm's study, *Calvin and The Calvinists* (Edinburgh/Carlisle, PA: The Banner of Truth Trust, 1982).

to the Regulative Principle of worship, maintaining the ongoing relevance of moral law of God (including the fourth commandment on the Sabbath), and affirming covenant theology. Thus, it is possible that one could be considered "Reformed" in his soteriology (holding to the doctrines of grace) but not consistently Reformed in other areas of his theology and practice.

Some Presbyterian and other Reformed paedobaptists (those who believe and practice infant baptism) have suggested that one cannot be fully and consistently "Reformed" in theology, unless he holds to paedobaptism (infant baptism), as did the original Protestant reformers (like Calvin).[4] Contemporary Reformed Baptists, however, would protest this position, contending that one may be fully Reformed, while also affirming and practicing credo-baptism (believer's baptism). Reformed Baptists embrace a historic, robust confession, in the Second London [Baptist] Confession of Faith (1689).[5] Malaysian pastor and theologian Boon-Sing Poh suggests that this confession was "the most mature of the Confessions of Faith that came out of the Reformation."[6] In his study of the doctrine of the church among the early English Particular Baptists (i.e., confessional Baptists who held

---

[4] This argument is made in R. Scott Clark, *Recovering the Reformed Confession: Our Theology, Piety, and Practice* (Philipsburg, NJ: P&R, 2008). See also the debate in Matthew C. Bingham, et al, *On Being Reformed: Debates Over a Theological Identity* (Cham, Switzerland: Palgrave Pivot, 2018).

[5] The Second London [Baptist] Confession (referred to as 2LCF) was written in 1677 but only widely adopted and published by English Particular Baptists after 1689. It is based on the Westminster Confession of Faith (1646) and the Savoy Declaration (1658). This confession was adopted and published by these Baptists in part to demonstrate their essential solidarity with English Reformation theology. For a contemporary analysis of this confession, see James M. Renihan, *To the Judicious and Impartial Reader: An Exposition of the 1689 London Baptist Confession of Faith* (Cape Coral, Florida: Founders Ministries, 2022. Published in the UK as *Confessing the Faith*, vol 2, *The Second London Baptist Confession of Faith*, (Macclesfield, UK: Broken Wharfe, 2022).

[6] Boon-Sing Poh, *The Fundamental of our Faith: Studies on the 1689 Baptist Confession of Faith* (Damansara Utama, Malaysia: Good News Enterprise, 2017), xx.

to "particular redemption," one of the five doctrines of grace discussed below), historian James M. Renihan argues that these men "believed that they had taken the principles of the Reformation to their proper conclusion." He even suggests that in terms of recovering the gospel and the Scriptural patterns of church order, "they were self-consciously more reformed than the paedobaptist reformed churches." Renihan thus concludes one can, in fact, be consistently Reformed in theology and also hold to a credo-baptist position. [7]

Whatever one's view of what constitutes Reformed theology, the doctrines of grace are clearly an essential and distinguishing component of it. One might hold to the doctrines of grace and not be fully Reformed, but one cannot be fully Reformed and reject the doctrines of grace.

A System of Theology

The doctrines of grace are a theological or doctrinal system, consisting of five basic affirmations. The five affirmations or "points" (referred to above as "the five points of Calvinism") are also commonly known by the acronym TULIP:

T—Total Depravity;
U—Unconditional Election;
L—Limited Atonement;
I—Irresistible Grace;
P—Perseverance of the Saints.

It should be stressed again that these five points are really five interrelated sub-doctrines of the larger doctrine of salvation (soteriology). These

---

[7] James M. Renihan, *Edification and Beauty: The Practical Ecclesiology of the English Particular Baptists, 1675–1705* (Milton Keynes, UK: Paternoster Press, 2008), 17.

five points are an attempt to understand how God is pleased to save sinners through Christ. The doctrines of grace stress man's spiritual inability due to the total impact of sin (T); God's plan to save the elect in Christ (U); God's particular work of redemption for the elect in Christ's death on the cross (L); the effectiveness of God's grace in applying redemption to the elect (I); and God's ability to keep the elect in a state of grace (P).

Joel Beeke offers the following succinct summary of the five points:

Total depravity (sovereign grace needed): man is so depraved and corrupted by sin in every part of his being that he is by nature incapable of doing any spiritual good and cannot affect any part of his salvation (Gen. 6:5);

Unconditional election (sovereign grace conceived): from eternity past, God chose to save certain individuals irrevocably to everlasting life and glory in Christ Jesus without seeing any intrinsic goodness in them, and He ordained the means by which they would be saved (Rom. 9:15–16);

Limited atonement (sovereign grace merited): while the death of Christ is sufficient to cover the sins of the world, its saving efficacy is intentionally limited to His elect sheep whose sins He bore and for whom He fully satisfied the justice of God (John 17:9);

Irresistible grace (sovereign grace applied): God irresistibly calls the elect to saving faith and salvation in Christ with such sovereign power that they can no longer resist His grace, but are made willing in the day of His power (Ps. 110:3; John 6:44–45); and,

Perseverance (sovereign grace preserved): those whom God saves, He graciously preserves in the state of grace so that they will never be lost. They may be troubled by infirmities as they seek to make their calling and election sure, but they will persevere until the end, fighting the good fight of faith until the final victory shall be realized in the coming again of their Savior and Lord as Judge (John 10:28).[8]

One will sometimes hear people say that they hold to some of these five doctrines but not to all. Many Baptists (excluding so-called "Free Will" Baptists), for example, will at least say that they hold to some form of the "P" ("Perseverance of the Saints") of TULIP, even if they distort the classical expression of the doctrine and call it "once saved always saved" or "eternal security."[9] One will sometimes hear a person claim to be a "three point" or "four point" Calvinist, indicating that he holds to several of the points but not to all five. There is a logical problem, however, with the notion that one might hold to some of the five points and not to all, since each is inextricably connected to the others. The five points are like five foundational pillars upholding the "structure" of the Reformed doctrine of salvation. Taking one point away would create a "domino-effect" which would pull down all the others and bring about the collapse of the entire system.

---

[8] From Joel R. Beeke, *The Heritage Reformed Congregations: Who We Are and What We Believe* (Grand Rapids, MI: Reformation Heritage Books, 2007), 11.
[9] Neither of these terms accurately reflects or articulates the Reformed doctrine of the perseverance of the saints and are not used by those who hold to the doctrines of grace. See chapter 5 on this doctrine.

Some will also perhaps say they desire to eschew the terminology of Calvinism and to be simple Biblicists, free from any "man-made" systematic approach. Such persons overlook several important facts. First, human beings have a tendency to think in orderly ways, which reflects the fact that we have been made in the image of a consistent and orderly God (see 1 Cor. 14:33). Though our reason has been tainted by sin (see "T"), we retain a rational capacity. They fail to see that the doctrines of grace, rightly used, are not an attempt to impose a system on Scripture but to make sense of what Scripture itself systematically teaches. Second, those who dismiss all systematic approaches also dismiss the fact that God was pleased to use human means to write the Scriptures and wanted them to be clearly understood by those who read them. If we deny that we can take distinct doctrines from the Bible, we deny that the Scriptures are clear and that the Spirit has effectively made doctrine known within them.

Furthermore, those who denounce efforts at a systematic approach to interpreting Scripture must explain why God would be more glorified by disorganized and contradictory thinking than by organized and harmonious thinking. Many of those who denounce clearly defined structures, in fact, operate within highly developed systems of doctrines and interpretations that are merely left unstated and unwritten. Fundamentally, their problem with the doctrines of grace is not with the fact that it is a "human" interpretation of Scripture but that it contradicts their own "human" interpretation of Scripture.

Andrew Fuller (1754–1815) was a key English Calvinistic Baptist Pastor and one of the founders of the Baptist Missionary Society that sent William Carey to India as one of the first "foreign" missionaries. Regarding the importance of clear and systematic understandings of biblical doctrines, Fuller wrote:

The man who has no creed has no belief; which is to say the same thing as an unbeliever; and he whose belief is not formed into a system has only a few loose, unconnected thoughts, without entering into the harmony and glory of the gospel. Every well-informed and consistent believer, therefore, must have a creed—a system which he supposes to contain the leading principles of Divine revelation.[10]

In the mid-nineteenth century, the so-called "Campbellite" movement arose in America, led by the Scottish minister Alexander Campbell (1788–1866). Those in this movement piously claimed to be restoring primitive Christianity by rejecting "human creeds." Campbell and his followers wanted, "No creed but Christ, no law but love, no book but the Bible." The Campbellites were not merely *non-creedal* but passionately *anti-creedal*. Among the defenders of confessional Christianity who arose to answer Campbell was the Southern Presbyterian theologian Robert Lewis Dabney (1820–1898). Dabney vigorously defended the proper use of creeds:

As man's mind is notoriously fallible, and professed Christians who claim to hold to the Scriptures, as they understand them, differ from each other notoriously, some platform for union or cooperation must be adopted, by which those who believe they are truly agreed may stand and work together. It is the only possible expedient, in the absence of an inspired living umpire, such as the pope claims falsely to be, by which fidelity to truth can be reconciled with cooperation. A creed, then, is such a means for enabling Christians to understand each

---

[10] Andrew Fuller, "Creeds and Subscriptions," in *The Complete Works of the Rev. Andrew Fuller*, vol. 3 (Harrisonburg, VA: Sprinkle Publications, 1988), 449.

other. It is the human exposition of what is supposed to be the exact meaning of the Scriptures; and differs from those usually delivered from the pulpit only in being more carefully and accurately made by the assistance of many minds. Its setting forth is an exercise of the church's ordinary didactic function. It must advance nothing which its compilers do not suppose to be fully sustained by the Scriptures; and no authority is claimed for it, in any respect, save that which they believe is communicated by the word of God.[11]

Dabney was primarily defending the use of the Westminster Standards (the Presbyterian confessional documents, consisting of the *Westminster Confession of Faith* and the *Larger* and *Shorter Catechism*). However, his words might well be marshalled in defence of the articulation of the doctrines of grace themselves as a coherent system.

In his classic devotional work on spiritual depression, Dr Martyn Lloyd-Jones diagnosed a lack of interest in doctrine as a root of spiritual problems for many discontented Christians, who claim they need only the Bible. To those people, Lloyd-Jones responds, "But what is the purpose of the Bible but to present doctrine? What is the value of exposition unless it leads to the truth?" Lloyd-Jones thus commended the use of creeds and confessions, noting:

The whole purpose of all the creeds drawn up by the Christian Church, together with every confession of faith on doctrine and dogma was to enable people to see and think clearly. . . So, if we object to doctrine it is not surprising if we do not

---

[11] Robert Lewis Dabney, "The System of Alexander Campbell: An Examination of Its Leading Points", in *Dabney's Discussions*, vol. 1 (Harrisonburg, VA: Sprinkle Publications, 1992), 315, first published in *Southern Presbyterian Review* (July, 1880).

see things clearly, it is not surprising if we are unhappy and miserable. There is nothing that so clears a man's spiritual sight as the apprehension and understanding of the doctrines of the Bible.[12]

His point: there are practical, spiritual benefits to confessional Christianity. A biblical creed outlines the doctrines that the Christian needs for spiritual health and happiness.

We agree with Fuller, Dabney, and Lloyd-Jones that to hold to a well-thought-out theological system as articulated in a well-written creed or confession is not a sign of compromise or downgrade but a mark of integrity, fidelity, and even of spiritual health. Any system must, of course, always be open to verification based on Scriptural argument and evidence. Those who hold to the doctrines of grace are confident that these doctrines will withstand the scrutiny of those who measure them by the standard of Scripture.[13]

The Rise, Fall, and Revival of the Doctrines of Grace

We noted above the rediscovery of and emphasis on the doctrine of salvation during the Protestant Reformation. When, however, was

---

[12] D. Martyn Lloyd-Jones, *Spiritual Depression: Its Causes and Cure* (Grand Rapids, MI: Eerdmans, 1965), 45–46.

[13] For a brief exposition of the Doctrines of Grace which avoids theological jargon while relying primarily on scriptural proofs, see D. Scott Meadows, *God's Astounding Grace* (North Bergen, NJ: Pillar and Ground, 2012). The subtitle for this booklet is, "The Doctrines of Grace Simply Explained from Scripture for Berean Christians." Meadows does not even explicitly use the TULIP acronym. Chapter titles (with corresponding TULIP references added) include:

Our Need of Grace (T)

The Election of Grace (U)

The Price of Grace (L)

The Attraction of Grace (I)

The Triumph of Grace (P)

TULIP explicitly articulated? The "five points" of Calvinism emerged as a response to what might be called the "five points" of Arminianism. James Arminius (or Jacob Hermann, 1560–1609) was a Dutch pastor and humanist scholar who sought to temper the Reformed doctrine of salvation as taught by John Calvin and his followers. Arminius gained a number of followers, who came to be known as "Arminians." In 1610 these men issued the "Arminian Remonstrance" to the Dutch Parliament which included five statements reflecting the teaching of Arminius. They can be summarized as falling under the following headings:

Conditional election;
Unlimited atonement;
Sinfulness capable of being overcome;
Resistible (prevenient) grace;
Precariousness of the Saints.[14]

Calvin's followers responded by calling an international conference (including delegates from across Protestant Europe) which convened as the Synod of Dort (meeting in Dort or Dordrecht, Holland) from 1618–1619. The conference met for seven months (November 1618 to May 1619) in one hundred and fifty-four sessions and, in the end, issued a firm rebuke of each of the Arminian points. The five points of Arminianism were thus rejected under these five heads of doctrine:

Of Divine Predestination (Unconditional election);
Of the Death of Christ, and the Redemption of Men thereby (Limited Atonement);

---

[14] To read the Arminian articles in parallel columns of Dutch, Latin, and English, see Philip Schaff, *The Creeds of Christendom*, Vol. 3 (Grand Rapids, Mich.: Baker Books, 1998): 545–49.

Of the Corruption of Man (Total Depravity);
Of his conversion to God, and the Manner thereof (Irresistible Grace);
Of the Perseverance of the Saints.[15]

From these five points (with the Dortian order shuffled) came the TULIP designation, which continues in use today.

Among the doctrinal heirs of Arminianism are those in the Methodist (following John Wesley), Holiness, Pentecostal, "Free Will" Baptist, and Disciples of Christ movements. It is also prominent among most mainline Protestants. Among the heirs of Dortian Calvinism we could list the Dutch Reformed churches, Reformed Presbyterians, Calvinistic Methodists (like George Whitefield), historic Particular Baptists, modern Reformed Baptists, and various other Reformed churches.

Many early Baptists in America were explicitly Calvinistic in outlook. In 1742 the Philadelphia Baptist Association, the first Baptist association formed in America, adopted the Philadelphia Baptist Confession, a creed that warmly expounded the doctrines of grace.[16] This emphasis, however, eventually waned. Reformed Baptist theologian Samuel Waldron lists seven major factors for the decline of the doctrines of grace among Baptists in America, particularly in the nineteenth century,[17] including the rise of the

---

[15] Schaff, *Creeds*, 550–97.
[16] The Philadelphia Baptist Confession is identical with the Second London [Baptist] Confession (1689) with the addition of two articles, sanctioning hymn singing and the practice of the laying on of hands. See William L. Lumpkin, *Baptist Confessions of Faith* (Valley Forge, PA: Judson Press, 1969), 348–53. The English Baptists who wrote the Second London Confession modified the Presbyterian views of the Westminster Confession on baptism, church government, and the relationship between the church and state but not its classic reformation emphasis on the doctrines of grace.
[17] Samuel E. Waldron, *Baptist Roots in America* (Boonton, NJ: Simpson, 1991), 9–29

American democratic ethos,[18] the practice of revivalism, the success of Methodism,[19] "inclusivism" (the pragmatic effort to bridge the divide between Calvinists and Arminians), reaction against hyper-Calvinism, modernism, and the development of fundamentalism (which focused on various important "fundamental" biblical truths, like the historical reality of the virgin birth of Christ, rather than issues related to soteriology). By the mid-twentieth century all these factors and others had led to the serious decline of the preaching, teaching, and promotion of the doctrines of grace among Baptists, as well as among most other evangelical Christians and their churches.

Beginning in the mid-twentieth century, however, there was a marked renewal of interest in and revival of these doctrines. Presbyterian theologian J. Ligon Duncan has identified several key factors in this resurgence, including the influence of popular preachers and theologians like D. Martyn Lloyd-Jones and R. C. Sproul, the formation and development of publishing ministries like the Banner of Truth, and renewal movements among Protestant denominations in light of the decline of modern liberalism.[20] In recent decades the doctrines of grace have indeed found a ready hearing among many who have become disillusioned with what they perceive to be the pragmatism and doctrinal superficiality that characterizes so much of Protestant evangelicalism.

By the early 2000s young adults, in particular, began to embrace

---

[18] See also Nathan O. Hatch, *The Democratization of American Christianity* (New Haven, CT: Yale University Press, 1989).

[19] See Iain H. Murray, *Wesley and Men Who Followed* (Edinburgh/Carlisle, PA: Banner of Truth Trust, 2003).

[20] J. Ligon Duncan, "The Resurgence of Calvinism in America," in *Calvin for Today*, ed. Joel R. Beeke, (Grand Rapids, Mich.: Reformation Heritage, 2009), 227–240.

the doctrines of grace.[21] The cover article of the March 23, 2009 annual special issue of *Time Magazine* was titled "Ten Ideas Changing the World Right Now" and number three on the list was "The New Calvinism." In this article, David Van Biema wrote:

> Calvinism is back . . . . John Calvin's 16th century reply to medieval Catholicism's buy-your-way-out-of-purgatory excesses is Evangelicalism's latest success story, complete with an utterly sovereign and micromanaging deity, sinful and puny humanity, and the combination's logical consequence, predestination: the belief that before time's dawn, God decided whom he would save (or not), unaffected by any subsequent human action or decision.[22]

Jerry Walls and Joseph Dongell note that many of those drawn to Calvinism from non-Reformed evangelical churches "have observed that segments of their denomination, like much of American evangelicalism, have become theologically thin, spiritually superficial and morally confused" and concluded that "Arminian theology is a major (if not *the* major) cause of these ills."[23] For some the

---

[21] This trend was recognized by Colin Hansen in his book *Young, Restless, Reformed: A Journalist's Journey with the Young Calvinists* (Wheaton, IL: Crossway, 2008). The "New Calvinist" movement has been, however, uneven and often disappointing. For a friendly yet cautious assessment of this movement, see Jeremy Walker, *New Calvinism Considered: A Personal and Pastoral Assessment* (Darlington: Evangelical Press, 2013). For a more trenchant assessment, see E. S. Williams, *The New Calvinists: Changing the Gospel* (London: Wakeman Trust & Belmont House Publishing, 2014).
[22] David Van Biema, "Ten Ideas Changing the World Right Now," in *Time Magazine* 173, no. 12 (March 23, 2009). https://content.time.com/time/specials/packages/article/0,28804,1884779_1884782_1884760,00.html
[23] Jerry L. Walls and Joseph R. Dongell, *Why I Am Not a Calvinist* (Downers Grove, IL: InterVarsity Press, 2004), 15. See also the counter-perspective to Walls and Dongell in Robert A. Peterson and Michael D. Williams, *Why I Am Not an Arminian*, (Downers Grove, IL: InterVarsity Press, 2004).

enchantment with the doctrines of grace as an alternative to evangelical superficiality has proven to be only a passing fad on the way to some new destination.[24] Others, however, have moved beyond merely seeing Calvinism as the right understanding of salvation to embracing all aspects of Reformed confessionalism. After a long season of distinct decline, all observers would agree that the doctrines of grace have re-emerged in the mainstream of traditional and evangelical Christianity.

Conclusion

The doctrines of grace are a systematic exposition, rooted in history, of Paul's affirmation that "by grace are ye saved through faith" (Eph. 2:8). These doctrines boldly affirm with Jonah that "Salvation is of the LORD" (Jonah 2:9) and with John that "We love him, because he first loved us" (1 John 4:19). Charles H. Spurgeon described the five points of Calvinism as "five great lamps which help to irradiate the cross; or, rather, five bright emanations springing from the glorious covenant of our Triune God."[25] The doctrines of grace are indeed an exposition of the biblical gospel. Men are sinners who deserve God's wrath and punishment, but God sent his Son to save sinners. These doctrines were reclaimed during the Reformation period, largely neglected during the nineteenth century, but revived in recent times. These great doctrines continue to encourage, excite, and embolden those who discover and embrace them.

---

[24] For an example of an "ex-Calvinist" see Austin Fischer, *Young, Restless, No Longer Reformed: Black Holes, Love, and a Journey In and Out of Calvinism* (Eugene, OR: Cascade Books, 2014). For my review of this work see *Puritan Reformed Journal* 7, no. 2 (July 2015), 277–279.
[25] C. H. Spurgeon. *Autobiography,* vol. 2, *The Full Harvest* (1900, repr., Edinburgh/Carlisle, PA: Banner of Truth, 1973), 12.

Chapter 1
TOTAL DEPRAVITY

In the introduction we offered a brief overview of the doctrines of grace, noting the popular acronym TULIP to summarize the "five points of Calvinism." This chapter will examine the "T" in TULIP, which stands for the doctrine of "Total Depravity." Some prefer to call this doctrine "radical depravity" or "pervasive depravity." The doctrine of Total Depravity maintains that the extent of the spiritual impact of sin since the fall in Genesis 3 is so pervasive in mankind as to make man's salvation completely dependent on the work of God alone.[26] God alone is responsible for saving men, because man in his sinful, unregenerate state will not choose Christ apart from God's own gracious intervention.

This doctrine takes seriously the hideous nature of human sinfulness. Those who are not believers generally hold an optimistic view of human nature. They believe that people are basically good and are only corrupted due to the influence of culture or environment. The biblical view, however, is that men are sinners who, if left to their own devices, will invariably reject God. This propensity toward sin impacts every area of life.

In the political sphere, this means that human societies have need of competent civil authority for good government to restrain evil (see Rom. 13:1–4). Christians are always sceptical, therefore, of utopian

---

[26] The terms "mankind" and "man" are used inclusively throughout this work to refer to all human beings, both male and female.

visions of human society free from godly order, authority, and restraint. One vivid example comes to mind. A few years ago, in the university town of Charlottesville, Virginia, the progressive city council decided to set up free bike racks, stocked with bright yellow "loaner" bikes at key locations throughout the city. The idea was that citizens could borrow a bike to ride from one part of the city to another, deposit the bike at a rack near their destination, and then pick up another for their ride to their next stop. It certainly sounded like a nice idea. The only problem was that it did not take human sin into consideration. Within a few days after the racks were put in place, nearly all the bikes were either stolen, broken, or left discarded throughout the city. Many were even tossed into a local river! The city council suffered from an over-optimistic view of human nature!

The key impact of sin, however, is not merely on the societal level but on the personal and individual level. Some naively hold that the only reason the unregenerate do not believe in Christ is simply because they have not yet heard a compelling-enough or culturally relevant gospel presentation about him. Church growth entrepreneurs have told us that non-believers are spiritual "seekers" who are eagerly trying to find God. The Bible, however, tells a far different and more disturbing story. Men may be spiritual seekers—in fact, Paul found the ancient city of Athens littered with pagan idols (see Acts 17:16–34)—but they are not seeking the jealous God of the Bible who demands righteousness and holiness. In Romans 3:11 Paul said, "There is none that understandeth, there is none that seeketh after God." He was describing the plight of the unregenerate man bound up in sin. The Bible holds out the scandalous truth that the only way a sinful man becomes a seeker of the one true God of the Bible is if God sovereignly opens the sinner's heart to receive the gospel. We can look to the description of the conversion of Lydia in Acts 16, "whose heart the Lord opened, that she attended unto the things which were spoken of Paul" (16:14b).

A clear articulation of the human condition in sin may be uncomfortable, but it is also truthful and realistic. Preachers must understand the wretchedness of man's condition apart from Christ, if they are rightly to preach the gospel. Sinners must hear the bad news of God's just wrath against sin and sinners, so that they might come to understand and appreciate the good news of God's love, mercy, and grace in Christ. Much evangelism today is offering the "cure" of God's love to a people who do not understand that they are dead in their sin and trespasses and deserving of divine wrath.[27] To recover biblical evangelism, we must correspondingly recover the biblical doctrine of total depravity.

Observations on the Doctrine of Total Depravity

To understand better man's need of Christ, we will offer seven observations on the doctrine of total depravity.

(1)TOTAL DEPRAVITY DOES NOT MEAN WE ARE NO LONGER GOD'S IMAGE-BEARERS.

Total depravity is sometimes maligned and mischaracterized as suggesting that sinful men are somehow sub-human, with the image of God completely defaced. Total depravity, however, is not *absolute depravity*. This doctrine does not hold that unregenerate men are the epitome of absolute evil. Though the image of God is tarnished in man, Scripture continues to speak of man as God's image-bearer, even after the fall (cf. Gen. 9:6; Ps. 8; James 3:9). Still, the Bible also teaches that the spiritual wounding of sin has made him completely incapable

---

[27] For a critique of superficial evangelism, see Walter Chantry, *Today's Gospel: Authentic or Synthetic?* (Edinburgh/Carlisle, PA: Banner of Truth, 1970).

of knowing the Lord apart from divine grace. In his *Institutes*, John Calvin observed, "Therefore, even though we grant that God's image was not totally annihilated and destroyed in him, yet it was so corrupted that whatever remains is frightful deformity."[28] Likewise, in his commentary on John 9:39 regarding Christ's healing of the man born blind, Calvin said:

> It is true that we are all born blind, but still, amidst the darkness of corrupt and depraved nature, some sparks continue to shine, so that men differ from brute beasts. Now, if any man, elated by proud confidence in his own opinion, refuses to submit to God, he will seem—apart from Christ—to be wise, but the brightness of Christ will strike him with dismay; for never does the vanity of the human mind begin to be discovered, until heavenly wisdom is brought into view.[29]

Though sin has gravely damaged all mankind, the image of God has not been completely removed. In his state of depravity, however, man cannot help himself and must depend upon God alone for salvation.

(2) TOTAL DEPRAVITY IMPACTS THE TOTALITY OF OUR BEING.

The terms "radical depravity" or "pervasive depravity" are perhaps most helpful in understanding the totality of Total Depravity. The English word "radical" comes from the Latin word *radix* meaning root or foundation. Sin reaches to our roots. Sin is foundational to understanding mankind's current condition in that sin impacts every

---

[28] John Calvin, *Institutes of the Christian Religion*, vol. 1, ed. John T. McNeil (Louisville: Westminster John Knox Press, 1960), 189.
[29] John Calvin, *Calvin's Commentaries*, Calvin Translation Society Edition, vol. 17, (Grand Rapids, MI: Baker Books, 2009), 391.

aspect of a person's being. It is pervasive in that its influence had spread throughout every part of who we are. Sin thus affects men physically, emotionally, rationally, intellectually, personally, politically, socially, and spiritually. There is no part of man that stands outside the shadow of sin's influence.

The prophet Jeremiah writes, "Can the Ethiopian change his skin, or the leopard his spots? then may ye also do good, that are accustomed to do evil." (Jer. 13:23). The Apostle Paul concurs when he declares, "For I know that in me (that is, in my flesh,) dwelleth no good thing: for to will is present with me; but how to perform that which is good I find not" (Rom. 7:18). These witnesses from the Old and New Testaments agree that sin is "radical" and "pervasive" in its presence and influence in mankind.

(3) Total Depravity is universal, impacting all men.
The Bible makes clear that sin is universal. In the days of Noah we read, "And God saw that the wickedness of man was great in the earth, and that every imagination of the thoughts of his heart was only evil continually" (Gen. 6:5). God summons the flood to wipe away mankind with its wickedness, preserving Noah and his family. Yet even after the flood, sin remained among the preserved remnant. When the Lord smelled the "sweet savour" of Noah's sacrifices offered after the flood, he said in his heart, "the imagination of man's heart is evil from his youth" (Gen. 8:21). The prophet Jeremiah likewise lamented: "The heart is deceitful above all things, and desperately wicked: who can know it?" (Jer. 17:9). In Romans 3:23, Paul offers this summation, "For all have sinned, and come short of the glory of God." Sin affects men of all nations, tribes, and tongues. It affects Jew and Gentile, male and female, high and low, young and old, healthy and sick, educated and uneducated. It is like a hidden and corrosive spiritual illness that infests each human being.

(4) Total Depravity means that men are sinners from
conception.

The Bible teaches that we inherit a sin nature at the very moment
of our conception. This sin nature can be traced back in unbroken
succession to our first parents, Adam and Eve. Paul states this clearly in
Romans 5, when he says, "For if by one man's offense death reigned by
one; much more they which receive abundance of grace and of the gift
of righteousness shall reign in life by one, Jesus Christ" (5:17; cf. Rom.
6:23). Sin came by one man's offense (Adam), and life by one man's
righteousness (Christ). Paul makes the same point in 1 Corinthians
15:20–22, noting that "For as in Adam all die, even so in Christ all
shall be made alive" (15:22). From Adam we all inherit a sin nature.
From Christ, however, we receive the promise of universal resurrection.
For some (the elect) this will be the resurrection to life, but for others
(the reprobate) it will be the resurrection of condemnation (see John
5:26–29).

Theologians have referred to the fact that men are sinners from
conception as "original sin." As one adage puts it, "We are not sinners
because we sin; we sin because we are sinners." For evidence of this
doctrine in Scripture compare:

Behold, I was shapen in iniquity; and in sin did my mother
conceive me (Ps. 51:5).

The wicked are estranged from the womb: they go astray as
soon as they be born, speaking lies (Ps. 58:3).

The Bible is clear that we do not merely become sinners when we
commit actual transgressions, but we are sinners from the moment of
conception, when we inherit and possess a sin nature.

(5) Total Depravity means that men are sinners not only by nature, but also because of their transgressions.

We are held to account not only for our inherited sin nature but also for our actual transgression of God's law in thought, word, and deed. This is found both in what we do (sins of commission) and fail to do (sins of omission). Every man is not only inclined toward sin, but given time and opportunity, he will all too readily break God's commands. In describing why the Suffering Servant came, Isaiah says, "All we like sheep have gone astray; we have turned every one to his own way; and the LORD hath laid on him the iniquity of us all" (Isa. 53:6). John notes, "If we say we have no sin, we deceive ourselves, and the truth is not in us" (1 John 1:8). Paul warned that we must all one day stand before "the judgment seat of Christ" to "receive the things done in his body, according to that he hath done, whether it be good or bad" (2 Cor. 5:10). Sin is not merely a theoretical principle but an actual and repeated occurrence in our lives.

(6) Total Depravity means that no sinner willingly chooses God, apart from regeneration.

This point was made in the introduction above, but it must be repeated here with emphasis. When the Lord Jesus spoke to Nicodemus, he said, "Verily, verily, I say unto thee, Except a man be born again, he cannot see the kingdom of God" (John 3:3). He then said to non-believers in John 5:40, "And ye will not come to me that ye might have life." A new birth experience, a change of nature (regeneration) is required before a person willingly turns to Christ.

It is sometimes falsely said that those who hold to the doctrines of grace do not believe in human free will. No. This is wrong. Calvinists believe in man's free will, but they also believe that man's will has been so corrupted by sin, that he will not choose Christ on his own, apart from God's grace. His damaged will must be renewed.

This was the teaching rediscovered by the Protestant Reformers. Martin Luther's classic doctrinal work was titled, *The Bondage of the Will*.[30] The Reformers maintained that salvation is not *synergistic*. Synergism was the view of the medieval Roman Catholic Church, that humans are saved by their cooperation with divine grace. The Reformers insisted instead that salvation is *monergistic*, a free act of God's grace alone. There is a place for the human response of faith, but this response is necessarily preceded by God's regenerating work. In this way, God alone gets all the glory for salvation.

Paul describes the spiritual dullness and deadness of those who are not in Christ in 1 Corinthians 2:14: "But the natural man receiveth not the things of the Spirit of God: for they are foolishness unto him: neither can he know them, because they are spiritually discerned." Similarly in 2 Corinthians 4:3–4, Paul states,

> But if our gospel be hid, it is hid to them that are lost: In whom the god of this world hath blinded the minds of them which believe not, lest the light of the glorious gospel of Christ, who is the image of God, should shine unto them.

Here Paul describes the blindness of man's sinful state, preventing him from seeing the light of the glory of Christ. This leads us to an understanding of *human inability*. Unregenerate men do not welcome Christ. As the apostle John put it: "And this is the condemnation, that

---

[30] Martin Luther, *The Bondage of the Will*, trans. J. I. Packer and O. R. Johnson (London: James Clarke, 1957). Luther's magnum opus was published under the Latin title *De Servo Arbitrio* and was a response to Erasmus's 1524 treatise *De Libero Arbitrio* (The Freedom of the Will).

light is come into the world, and men loved darkness rather than light, because their deeds were evil" (John 3:19). Apart from God's grace, an unregenerate sinner does not love the light, nor does he strive to obey God's law (see Paul's description of man's inner struggle with sin in Rom. 7:7–25).[31] Paul emphatically declares that the sinner neither seeks God nor desires to do good:

> As it is written, There is none righteous, no, not one: There is none who understandeth, there is none that seeketh after God. They are all gone out of the way, they are together become unprofitable; there is none that doeth good, no, not one. (Rom. 3:10–12)

In chapter nine, "Of Free Will," in the Second London [Baptist] Confession, this doctrine is summarized as follows: "Man, by his fall into the state of sin, has wholly lost all ability of will to any spiritual good accompanying salvation; so as a natural man, being altogether averse from that good, and dead in sin, is not able by his own strength to convert himself, or to prepare himself thereunto." (2LCF 9.2)[32] Apart from God's quickening we are spiritually dead and under God's wrath:

---

[31] There has been a long interpretive discussion as to the identity of the man to whom Paul refers in Romans 7. Is Paul describing the condition of an unregenerate sinner before salvation? Or, is he describing the condition of a regenerate man who is battling sin in the process of progressive sanctification? Whatever one's decision on this point, he cannot avoid Paul's portrait of the seriousness of sin. For a compelling discussion of this issue in Romans 7, see John Murray, *The Epistle to the Romans* (Grand Rapids, MI: Eerdmans, 1968, 1997), 256–259. Murray concludes that Paul describes his "pre-regenerate experience" in 7:7–13 and his experience "in the state of grace" in 7:14–25.

[32] *The Baptist Confession of Faith & The Baptist Catechism* (Birmingham, AL: Solid Ground Christian Books, 2010). This and other citations from the confession will be taken from this source.

> And you hath he quickened, who were dead in trespasses and sins; Wherein in time past ye walked according to the course of this world, according to the prince of the power of the air, the spirit that now worketh in the children of disobedience: Among whom also we all had our conversation in time past in the lusts of our flesh, fulfilling the desires of the flesh and of the mind; and were by nature the children of wrath, even as others. (Eph. 2:1–3)

These are painful realities for the believer to consider within himself, let alone to share with unregenerate sinners. The unregenerate man's flesh will revolt against the condemnation of what he perceives to be his innate spiritual goodness. Faithful gospel preachers, however, must not be like those condemned by Jeremiah: "They have healed the hurt of the daughter of my people slightly, saying, Peace, peace; when there is no peace" (Jer. 6:14). We must instead be bold and speak the truth in love about unregenerate man's condition in sin.

(7) TOTAL DEPRAVITY HIGHLIGHTS GOD'S HOLINESS IN THE FACE OF MAN'S SINFULNESS.

The Bible declares not only that God hates sin but that he also hates sinners. Psalm 5:5 declares, "thou hatest all workers of iniquity." Psalm 7:11 adds, "God is angry with the wicked every day." His eyes are too holy to look upon unrighteousness:

> Thou art of purer eyes than to behold evil, and canst not look on iniquity: wherefore lookest thou upon them that deal treacherously, and holdest thy tongue when the wicked devoureth the man that is more righteous than he? (Hab. 1:13)

In his masterful analysis of human depravity, titled *The Sinfulness of*

Sin, the Puritan Ralph Venning observes, "God hates man for sin. It is not only sin (Prov. 6:16, 19) but sinners that God hates, and that for sin. It is said of God that he hates the workers of iniquity (Ps. 5:5); not only the works of iniquity, but the workers of it."[33] The truth of Scripture is not that Christ saves us from ourselves. Rather, Christ saves us from experiencing the righteous wrath of God against us for our sin. In John 3:36 we read, "He that believeth on the Son hath everlasting life: and he that believeth not the Son shall not see life; but the wrath of God abideth on him." In Romans 5:9 Paul likewise gladly declares that "being now justified by his blood, we shall be saved from wrath through him [Jesus]."

Perhaps we are prone to such a low view of sin because we hold such a high view of ourselves and a correspondingly low view of God's holiness and his justice. Yet until we understand the magnitude of human sin, we will not perceive the magnitude of God's salvation through Christ.

Conclusion

Our study of the doctrines of grace has begun with reflection on our sinful human condition. Sin is no minor hurdle we must overcome with a little bit of God's help. It is an insurmountable obstacle that will only be overcome by God reaching down to lift us over it. As Philip P. Bliss's 1875 hymn puts it:

> *Guilty, vile, and helpless we,*
> *Spotless Lamb of God was He;*
> *Full atonement! Can it be?*
> *Hallelujah, what a Savior!*

---

[33] Ralph Venning, *The Sinfulness of Sin* (Edinburgh/Carlisle, PA: Banner of Truth, 1669 [original], 1993), 189.

An honest and sober reckoning of unregenerate man's plight in sin is a necessary starting point to understand properly the solution offered by God's grace in Christ.

Chapter 2
UNCONDITIONAL ELECTION

In the previous chapter we sketched the first of the five points of Calvinism: man's condition in sin (total depravity). In that chapter, we addressed how man's will has been so corrupted by sin that he is unable to choose God until and unless he experiences regeneration by God's grace. The only way the sin barrier may be overcome is by the intervention of God himself through his gracious plan of salvation. This brings the discussion, quite naturally, to the issue of God's election (choosing) of those who would be saved. The second of the five points of Calvinism stresses that if any man is saved it will be because God graciously elects or chooses him for salvation. What is more, God does this by his own sovereign choice, apart from any condition of merit, achievement, or accomplishment in the person who is saved. This means that God's election is unconditional (without conditions)!

What is the doctrine of election?

In contemporary English the word "election" usually refers to a political process. Voters "choose" or "elect" a leader. When I served as a missionary in Budapest, Hungary during the first years after the fall of communism (1990–1992), I was able to witness that nation participate in its first free political elections in over forty-five years. The biblical word election also means "choosing," but it refers to God's choosing of those who would be saved. In biblical election we might say that there is only one "Voter," and it is the Lord himself.

The biblical word for "to choose" is *eklegomai*. This verb is the root for the English word "eclectic." If a homeschooling parent has an "eclectic" curriculum it means she chooses from among many resources to create one course of study for her children. In biblical election, God graciously chooses to save many from among all the nations, tribes, and tongues of humanity to be joined to his one people through Christ.

Observations on the Doctrine of Unconditional Election

Having understood what election is, what does it mean that God's election is unconditional, or without conditions? To answer this, we must first make some observations regarding how God's sovereignty is related to the doctrine of Unconditional Election.

(1) UNCONDITIONAL ELECTION IS BUILT ON THE FOUNDATION OF GOD'S SOVEREIGNTY

The doctrine of God's sovereignty is the foundation for the doctrine of election. The Bible teaches that God is omnipotent (all-powerful), omniscient (all-knowing), omni-present (all-present or present everywhere), and omni-benevolent (all-good).

Given the reality of his sovereignty, the Bible affirms that nothing can frustrate God's will.[34] Human beings cannot frustrate his will. As Proverbs 19:21 puts it, "There are many devices in a man's heart; nevertheless the counsel of the LORD, that shall stand." Nations cannot frustrate his plans. In the days of the prophet Isaiah, when the Assyrians rose up against Israel, God declared, "Surely as I have thought, so shall

---

[34] For this discussion of God's sovereignty, I was helped by the Scripture summaries in Samuel Waldron, *A Modern Exposition of the 1689 Confession,* 3rd ed., (Darlington: Evangelical Press, 1989, 2005), 63–64.

it come to pass; and as I have purposed, so shall it stand" (Isa. 14:24). He then added, "For the LORD of hosts hath purposed, and who shall disannul it? and his hand is stretched out, and who shall turn it back?" (14:27). In Isaiah 46:10–11 the Lord declares that he knows "the end from the beginning, and from ancient times the things that are not yet done, saying, My counsel shall stand, and I will do all my pleasure . . . yea, I have spoken it, I will also bring it to pass; I have purposed it, I will also do it." The Psalmist declares, "But our God is in the heavens: he hath done whatsoever he hath pleased" (Ps. 115:3; cf. Ps. 135:6; Acts 15:18).

The Bible further affirms that God is sovereign over everything that happens within his creation—not only over the good things that happen but also over the evil things. Since he is omni-benevolent he is never the source of evil, but he does permit evil to further his own wise designs. As Isaiah puts it, he forms the light and creates darkness (Isa. 45:7). The prophet Amos, likewise, declares, "shall there be evil in a city, and the LORD hath not done it?" (Amos 3:6). When Joseph spoke to his brothers who had sold him into slavery, he announced to them, "But as for you, ye thought evil against me; but God meant it unto good" (Gen. 50:20). The New Testament equivalent is expressed by Paul in this well-loved affirmation: "And we know that all things work together for good to them that love God, to them who are the called according to his purpose" (Rom. 8:28). Even the evil of evils, the death of Christ upon the cross, came about "by the determinate counsel and foreknowledge of God" (Acts 2:23; cf. 4:27–28). What men meant for evil, God turned into the greatest good for his own glory and for the salvation of the elect.

Men may believe that they are acting independently, according to their own autonomous designs, free and apart from God's sovereign oversight and direction, but this is only an illusion. As Solomon observes, "A man's heart deviseth his way: but the LORD directeth his steps" (Prov. 16:9; cf. 16:1; 21:1). In Psalm 139 David declares that God knew him before he was formed in the womb and recorded all the days ordained for him in his book (139:16). God's sovereign governance extends to every aspect of our lives. Jesus himself taught that not even a sparrow falls in the field apart from God's will. Even the hairs on our heads are numbered by him (Matt. 10:29–30)!

(2) UNCONDITIONAL ELECTION HIGHLIGHTS GOD'S SOVEREIGNTY IN SALVATION

Having grasped the Bible's teaching on the sovereignty of God, we must then understand how that sovereignty is expressed in his election of those who will be saved. The precedent for this is set in God's election of Israel in the Old Testament:

> The LORD did not set his love upon you, nor choose you, because ye were more in number than any people; for ye were the fewest of all people: But because the LORD loved you, and because he would keep the oath which he had sworn unto your fathers, hath the LORD brought you out with a mighty hand, and redeemed you out of the house of bondmen, from the hand of Pharaoh king of Egypt. (Deut 7:7–8)

God did not choose Old Testament Israel to be his people because they were a numerous or strong people. They were not chosen because of their merit or accomplishments. God chose to set his affection upon Israel simply as an expression of his sovereign will. They became the objects of God's love because of God's sovereign choice alone.

God's election of Israel in the Old Testament is parallel with the way in which Jesus spoke of God's sovereign revelation of his identity to his disciples and of his election of his original disciples in the Gospels:

> All things are delivered unto me of my Father: and no man knoweth the Son, but the Father; neither knoweth any man the Father, save the Son, and he to whomsoever the Son will reveal him. (Matt. 11:27)

> Ye have not chosen me, but I have chosen you, and ordained you, that ye should go and bring forth fruit, and that your fruit should remain: that whatsoever ye shall ask of the Father in my name, he may give it you. (John 15:16)

The apostles and other New Testament authors likewise affirm the doctrine of sovereign election, as is evidenced in passages such as these (emphasis added):

> And when the Gentiles heard this, they were glad, and glorified the word of the Lord: *and as many as were ordained to eternal life believed.* (Acts 13:48)

> Be not thou therefore ashamed of the testimony of our Lord, nor of me his prisoner: but be thou partaker of the afflictions of the gospel according to the power of God; *Who hath saved us, and called us with an holy calling, not according to our works, but according to his own purpose and grace, which was given us in Christ Jesus before the world began*, But is now made manifest by the appearing of our Saviour Jesus Christ, who hath abolished death, and hath brought life and immortality to light through the gospel: Whereunto I am appointed a preacher, and an apostle, and a teacher of the Gentiles. (2 Tim. 1:8–11)

But we are bound to give thanks alway to God for you, brethren beloved of the Lord, because *God hath from the beginning chosen you to salvation through sanctification of the Spirit and belief of the truth*: Whereunto he called you by our gospel, to the obtaining of the glory of our Lord Jesus Christ. (2 Thess. 2:13–14)

Peter, an apostle of Jesus Christ, to the strangers scattered throughout Pontus, Galatia, Cappadocia, Asia, and Bithynia, *Elect according to the foreknowledge of God the Father*, through sanctification of the Spirit, unto obedience and sprinkling of the blood of Jesus Christ: Grace unto you, and peace, be multiplied. (1 Pet. 1:1–2)

In addition to the passages cited above, one should carefully examine two key passages in the writings of the apostle Paul: Romans 9:9–24 and Ephesians 1:1–12.

In Romans 9 Paul parallels God's choosing of the patriarch to continue the Abrahamic covenant, with election to salvation through Christ. He describes how Isaac's wife Rebecca had twins sons, Jacob and Esau, in her womb, but God sovereignly chose to continue his covenant through Jacob and not through Esau. God made this choice apart from any condition of merit fulfilled by Jacob or abrogated by Esau: "(For the children being not yet born, neither having done any good or evil, that the purpose of God according to election might stand, not of works, but of him that calleth;)" (Rom. 9:11). Thus, Paul can cite Malachi 1:2–3 in declaring: "As it is written, Jacob have I loved, but Esau have I hated" (9:13). Paul then anticipates those who might charge the Lord with unfairness or "unrighteousness": "What shall we say then? Is there unrighteousness with God? God forbid" (9:14). Paul again turns to the Old Testament Scriptures to cinch his point, citing the Lord's words to Moses in Exodus 33:19, "I will have mercy on whom I will have mercy, and I will have compassion on whom I will have compassion" (Rom. 9:15). This is nothing less than a declaration of the Godhood of God. To this Paul adds: "So then it is not of him that willeth, nor of him that runneth, but of God that sheweth mercy" (9:16). Notice the special stress here on the fact that salvation does not depend upon (or, is not conditioned upon) the will of man but upon the will of God. Sadly, many rush to defend the supposed sovereignty of the "free will" of fallen man and neglect the rightful biblical emphasis on the sovereign free will of God. So, Paul continues, "Therefore hath he mercy on whom he will have mercy, and whom he will he hardeneth" (9:18). Anticipating again the objections of those offended by divine sovereignty, "Why doth he yet find fault? For who hath resisted his will?" (9:19), Paul offers this correction: "Nay but, O man, who art thou that repliest against God? Shall the thing formed say to him that formed it, Why hast thou made me thus?" (9:20). Indeed, who is man, a limited creature, to question the wisdom of the sovereign Creator?

In Ephesians 1, likewise, Paul stresses God's sovereignty in election. His words are specifically addressed "to the saints which are at Ephesus, and to the faithful in Christ Jesus" (Eph. 1:1). To these saints Paul can say that God "hath chosen us in him before the foundation of the world, that we should be holy and without blame before him in love" (1:4). This choosing came by God's predestination or foreordination: "Having predestinated us unto the adoption of children by Jesus Christ to himself, according to the good pleasure of his will" (1:5). He did so to magnify his own glory: "To the praise of the glory of his grace, wherein he hath made us accepted in the beloved" (1:6). Now, he has made known to the saints, "the mystery of his will" (1:9).

The emphasis in these passages is on the fact that God's choosing is not "conditional" on any expected actions or responses of those who are saved, but it is an "unconditional" act of God's sovereign choice alone. We sometimes hear parents speak about their "unconditional love" for their children. This means that their children do not have to do or say anything to be loved. In a similar way, God's love for those who are saved is unconditional. He does not save individuals on the condition of their merit, their will, or even their belief, although those who have been saved will always respond in faith and repentance. How amazing and undeserved is this salvation, for which God alone deserves the glory!

Objections and queries about this doctrine

Having offered some discussion of the biblical doctrine of unconditional election, our focus now turns to challenges that might be raised against this doctrine. Here are nine such questions that are sometimes raised in objection, along with nine corresponding responses:

(1) Does election in the Bible refer to God's choosing of individuals to salvation or to something else?
This question often takes one of three forms:

First, some might ask, "Could passages that speak of God's choosing refer to the election of nations or believers as an undefined group and not to specific individuals?"

Response: Scripture clearly assumes that God's sovereignty extends not merely over corporate bodies but also over individuals (see again Prov. 16:9; Ps. 139:16; Matt. 10:30). When Paul says in Ephesians 1:4 "he hath chosen us," he was writing to a specific group (the saints at Ephesus; cf. Eph. 1:1), not to a generic or hypothetical audience. We should also not forget that groups and nations consist of individuals. Therefore, for God to elect a group of people is for him to elect the individuals within that group. It seems odd that some evangelicals who stress the importance of personal evangelism or "soul-winning" will make appeal to this argument, avoiding the most natural interpretation of the texts cited above. God chooses individuals for salvation!

Second, some might ask, "Could these passages refer to God's election (choosing) of Christ?"

Response: It is clear from Scripture that Christ, as the second person of the Godhead, is chosen and appointed to redeem his people through his incarnation, according to the covenant of redemption. However, the language of election is applied repeatedly and specifically in Scripture to the people who are to be redeemed.

Third, some might ask, "Could these passages refer to God's election of believers to sanctification and not to salvation?" In this regard, particular appeal is sometimes made to Romans 8:29 which speaks of believers being predestined "to be conformed to the image of his Son."

Response: It is agreed that full sanctification (known as glorification) is the final stage of salvation. All those who are saved eventually enter into the glorified state commencing either at their deaths or at the Lord's coming. All things will find their ultimate consummation at the second coming of Christ, the final resurrection, and the final judgment. In places like Romans 8:29–30 (the so-called "golden chain of redemption"), Paul is addressing the order of salvation, which includes final sanctification (glorification). The process of sanctification, however, does not proceed until one is saved. So, the issue of election to sanctification for the believer cannot be used to sidestep the other necessary aspects of the order of salvation, including divine foreknowledge and predestination (election to salvation).

In the end, none of these three challenges proves to be a "defeater" to the understanding of unconditional election as referring to the divine choosing of particular individuals (not nameless, face-less groups) to salvation (not merely to sanctification).

(2) DOES ELECTION MEAN THAT GOD'S CHOICE IS MERELY RANDOM?

Some critics have falsely described the doctrines of grace as like a version of the children's game: "Duck, Duck, Goose!" with the God of Calvinism making it "Duck, Duck, Damned!" Scripture affirms, however, that God's choices are never arbitrary. God's election is according to his own most-wise purposes and counsels. Even when his actions are mysterious to us, they are known to him (Deut. 29:29). Indeed, many things are often hidden from us, but we trust that all God's decisions tend toward the end of his own ultimate glory. The Lord spoke through the prophet Isaiah, saying, "For my thoughts are not your thoughts, neither are your ways my ways, saith the LORD. For as the heavens are higher than the earth, so are my ways higher than your ways, and my thoughts than your thoughts" (Isa. 55:8–9). The pagan king Nebuchadnezzar, after being humbled by God, likewise affirmed, "And all the inhabitants of the earth are reputed as nothing: and he doeth according to his will in the army of heaven, and among the inhabitants of the earth: and none can stay his hand, or say unto him, What doest thou?" (Dan. 4:35). God's election, therefore, is not purposeless or random but according to his perfect wisdom.

(3) COULD IT BE THAT GOD SIMPLY FOREKNOWS THOSE WHO WILL FREELY CHOOSE CHRIST AND THEN ELECTS THEM?

According to this view, it is not that God sovereignly decreed the salvation of the elect in eternity past, but that he simply looked down the corridors of time and foreknew those who would, in time, choose to believe the gospel. This would mean that God's election is conditioned upon man's election. Those who hold this view sometimes make appeal to Romans 8:29, which says, "For whom he did foreknow, he also did predestinate. . . ."

In response, the point first needs to be made that "foreknowledge" in Romans 8:29 does not merely refer to awareness of future factual events but to relationships. The Bible speaks, for example, of a man "knowing" a woman. For example, we see in Genesis 4:1: "But Adam knew Eve his wife. . . ." This does not mean that he possessed factual information about her actions, but that he had an intimate relationship with her. When the Bible speaks of God having "knowledge or foreknowledge" it does not always merely refer to his having an exhaustive factual understanding of events or actions. Instead, it often refers to his possession of an intimate relationship with persons. This distinction should guide one's interpretation of Romans 8:29. The Lord did merely possess factual information about who the elect might be, but he savingly knew each one of them.

In the end, the "foreknowledge explanation" really does not resolve the perceived problem of divine responsibility for salvation for the Arminian. If God simply factually foreknows that some will believe in Christ while others will reject Christ, why does he not alter circumstances so that those who reject him will instead respond in faith to Christ? Even if one were to accept this scheme, the responsibility for salvation would still remain firmly with God alone. That one must reject this scheme altogether, however, is made plain by Romans 9:11.

As previously noted, God chose to continue his covenant through Jacob and not through Esau, "neither having done any good or evil, that the purpose of God according to election might stand, not of works, but of him that calleth" (Rom. 9:11). God did not choose Jacob, because he foresaw anything good in him. He chose Jacob, because he is God.

(4) WHAT ABOUT THOSE WHO ARE NOT SAVED?

There are at least two views offered in response to this question.

The first view holds that God *actively* elects persons both to salvation and damnation (cf. John 12:37–40; Rom. 9:22–23; 2 Tim. 2:20; 1 Pet. 2:7–8; Jude 1:4). God elects (chooses) both the saved and the reprobate. This is sometimes referred to as "double predestination."

The second view suggests that there is a fundamental difference in God's election of the redeemed to salvation versus his election of the reprobate to damnation. God is *active* in electing the saved but merely *passive* in allowing the wicked to persist in their sinfulness (see Rom. 1:24; Eph. 4:17–19). Those who reject Christ are not actively damned by God, but they are passed over and left in their self-chosen sins, and ultimately are justly condemned for those sins. This view is reflected in Chapter three "Of God's Decree" in the Second London [Baptist] Confession, which state that some are predestined to eternal life to the praise of his glorious grace while others are "left to act in their sin to their just condemnation to the praise of his glorious justice" (2LCF 3.3).

Regardless of which view one takes, all agree that God is ultimately glorified in both the reprobate and the redeemed. The reprobate are the fit objects of God's wrath and glorify God's justice for eternity. The redeemed, however, glorify both the justice of God, as their sins have been laid upon Christ, and his gracious mercy, as they have been saved through no merit of their own.

(5) IS THIS DOCTRINE UNFAIR?

Those who raise this question as an objection sometimes do so based on two false assumptions. On one hand, they assume that there are people who want to be saved but who are not saved, simply because God did not choose them. This view does not take seriously the damage that sin has done to the spiritual life of mankind. No sinner wants to be saved unless God first changes his heart. Paul notes that apart from God's grace "there is none that seeketh after God" (Rom. 3:11).

On the other hand, some suggest that the doctrine of election means there are people who do not want to be saved, but who are saved nonetheless, contrary to their desires. Again, such hypothetical persons do not exist. No one is pulled kicking and screaming into the kingdom of God. Once a sinner experiences the new birth he gladly trusts and follows Christ.

As noted above, the apostle Paul anticipated the charge of unfairness in Romans 9:14: "What shall we say then? Is there unrighteousness with God? God forbid." The fundamental problem with the fairness argument is that it places a human view of justice above the revelation of God's sovereignty. Scripture affirms the Godhood of God. Whatever God chooses to do is by definition the standard of everything that is good, right, just, and true. Look once more at the words of Nebuchadnezzar: "and none can stay his hand, or say unto him, What doest thou?" (Dan. 4:35b) and consider again Paul's silencing of his critics with these words: "Nay but, O man, who art thou that repliest against God? Shall the thing formed say to him that formed it, Why hast thou made me thus?" (Rom. 9:20; cf. Job 9:12; Eccles. 8:4).

(6) What about human responsibility?

Some may object that the doctrine of election is not consistent with the concept of human responsibility. If the reprobate are pre-ordained for damnation, how can they be held responsible for their rejection of Christ? On this point, however, we must remember the biblical teaching on unregenerate man's pervasive depravity. The Second London Baptist Confession affirms that in God's decree no "violence" is "offered to the will of the creature" (2LCF 3.1); that is, God does not force man to do anything against his will. The reprobate are completely responsible for their own actions. They pay the due penalty for their sin. The sinner is responsible for his own sin and his own rejection of Christ.

On the other hand, the doctrine of election does not mean that the redeemed do not exercise personal responsibility in salvation. Those whom God chooses to save have their fallen wills renewed through regeneration. By the grace of God, they repent and believe in Christ. They are justified by their faith. When they believe in Christ, however, they confess that God alone deserves all the glory and praise for their salvation.

(7) Could God have intentionally limited his sovereign will so man could freely choose him?

First, this is essentially a hypothetical and man-centred philosophical argument rather than a biblical one. Nowhere in Scripture do we find the concept of God's self-limitation with regard to salvation. Thus, this theory has no biblical basis or framework. In addition, it would present a God whose knowledge of future events would be "open" or contingent on human actions. Thus, it would run counter to classical views of God as sovereign, all-knowing, and unchangeable (Mal. 3:6; James 1:17).

Second, this view presumes an overly optimistic view of man's free will. It presumes that sinful, unregenerate men would, of their own free will, seek to know, trust, and worship the God of the Bible. Scripture notes that no man, in his current sinful condition, will freely choose to bend the knee before the God of the Bible. As a proverb in 1 Samuel 24:13 puts it, "Wickedness proceedeth from the wicked." Why would we expect anything different to happen with regard to salvation?

(8) Does this doctrine create pride in those who believe they are among the elect?

This is certainly possible. Pride is a fundamental sin in all men, even among those who are converted. The doctrine of election properly understood, however, does little to promote pride in those who rightly understand it. The believer who affirms this doctrine knows that he was not saved because of any merit in himself, but purely through the grace of God. He was not more intelligent, more spiritual, or more upright than other men. He was simply the unworthy object of Christ's affection. Thus, right understanding of this doctrine actually deposes pride and develops proper humility in the Christian's heart (c.f. 1 Pet. 5:5-6).

(9) Will this doctrine dull the believer's zeal for evangelism?

Scripture teaches that God not only ordains the recipients of salvation in election, but he also ordains the means for their salvation. In Romans 10:14-15 Paul gave this charge to preach the gospel:

> How then shall they call on him in whom they have not believed? and how shall they believe in him of whom they have not heard? and how shall they hear without a preacher? And

how shall they preach, except they be sent? as it is written, How beautiful are the feet of them that preach the gospel of peace, and bring glad tidings of good things! (Rom. 10:14–15)

The apostle then adds: "So then faith cometh by hearing, and hearing by the word of God" (Rom. 10:17). All those who are chosen for salvation must first have the gospel preached to them, so that they might hear and believe in Christ. The effect of this preaching on the hearts of sinners is in God's hands. We do not know who will respond to the gospel. We do not choose who will be saved. We discover those whom God has chosen as we watch the elect respond in faith to gospel preaching.

In the Great Commission (Matt. 28:19–20), Christ ordered his disciples to go and teach (make disciples of) all nations, baptizing them in the name of the triune God, and teaching them to observe all of the Lord's commandments. The doctrine of election, far from quenching zeal for evangelism, gives us great confidence and boldness that we will be successful in this task. Many of the greatest cross-cultural, pioneer missionaries in Christian history have been those who have held to these doctrines, including William Carey, father of the modern evangelical missions movement and the first to take the gospel to India. If we faithfully preach Christ, God himself will be pleased to draw all kinds of men to himself (see John 12:32).

Conclusion and Caution

The doctrine of election is the biblical teaching that God himself chooses those who will be saved. We see this doctrine throughout Scripture. It is plainly referred to in places like Paul's letter to the Ephesians when he spoke of the believers being blessed with every blessing in Christ "According as he hath chosen us in him before the foundation of the world, that we should be holy and without blame before him in love: Having predestinated us unto the adoption of children by Jesus Christ to himself, according to the good pleasure of his will" (Eph. 1:4–5). This doctrine gives us boldness and confidence in sharing the good news of Christ, knowing there are many set apart by God himself for salvation.

This doctrine must be held with care and caution, however, knowing that we, as human beings, are not privy to all the mysteries bound up in the counsels of God. In John Bunyan's allegory *The Holy War* there is a scene in which Mr. Conscience is given the task of being a preacher to the citizens of the town of "Mansoul." Prince Emmanuel exhorts him: "but thou must not attempt to presume to be the revealer of those high and supernatural mysteries that are kept close to the bosom of Shaddai, my Father: for those things knows no man, nor can any reveal them but my Father's Secretary [the Holy Spirit] only."[35] The final paragraph in the Second London [Baptist] Confession's statement on God's decrees offers a similar caution all should heed:

> The doctrine of this high mystery of predestination is to be handled with special prudence and care, that men attending the will of God revealed in his Word, and yielding obedience thereunto, may, from the certainty of their effectual vocation, be assured of their eternal election; so shall this doctrine afford matter of praise, reverence, and admiration of God, and of humility, diligence, and abundant consolation to all that sincerely obey the gospel. (2 LCF 3.7)

---

[35] John Bunyan, *The Holy War* (Grand Rapids, MI: Baker Books, 1682, original; reprint 1978), 173.

Calvin himself warned against excessive "human curiosity" with regard to predestination (election). He noted that, "If allowed [such curiosity] will leave no secret to God which it will not search out and unravel." So, Calvin urged believers to avoid "wanton curiosity." On the other hand, however, he also noted that some "all but require that every mention of predestination be buried; indeed, they teach to avoid any question of it, as he would a reef." Calvin concludes, "Let us, I say, permit the Christian man to open his mind and ears to every utterance of God directed to him, provided it be with such restraint that when the Lord closes his holy lips, he shall also at once close the way to inquiry."[36] We, therefore, should approach the doctrine of God's unconditional election with humility, gratitude, and awe.

---

[36] The quotations from Calvin cited here are found in Edwin H. Palmer, *The Five Points of Calvinism,* enlarged ed. (Grand Rapids, MI: Baker Books, 1980), 118–19. They are taken from *Calvin's Institutes* 3.21.1–4.

Chapter 3
LIMITED ATONEMENT

The hymn writer Samuel J. Stone penned these words:

The Church's one foundation is Jesus Christ her Lord;
She is his new creation, by water and the Word:
From heav'n he came and sought her to be his holy bride,
with his own blood he bought her, and for her life he died.

What do we really mean when we read or sing the last line of that stanza: "with his own blood he bought her and for her life he died"? Did the Lord Jesus Christ really purchase his bride, the church, with his own blood on the cross, or did he only *potentially* redeem his bride? This question is central to the doctrine of Limited Atonement, a teaching which just might be the most controversial of the doctrines of grace and which some find least tenable. Among the Puritans, for example, Richard Baxter did not hold to Limited Atonement.[37]

It might help once again to review the doctrines of grace, using the acronym TULIP:

---

[37] See James I. Packer, "Introduction," Richard Baxter, *The Reformed Pastor*, ed. William Brown, (Edinburgh/Carlisle, PA: Banner of Truth, 1989), 9–19. Packer explains, "Baxter was a big man, big enough to have big faults and make big errors. . .. In theology, for instance, he devised an eclectic middle route between the Reformed, Arminian and Roman doctrines of grace: interpreting the kingdom of God in terms of contemporary political ideas, he explained Christ's death as an act of universal redemption (penal and vicarious, but not substitutionary), in virtue of which God made a new law offering pardon and amnesty to the penitent" (9–10).

T—Total depravity (sovereign grace needed)
U—Unconditional election (sovereign grace conceived)
L—Limited Atonement (sovereign grace merited)
I—Irresistible Grace (sovereign grace applied)
P—Perseverance of the Saints (sovereign grace preserved)

Once again, we should also note that these five points stand or fall together. There is a logical agreement that binds them together. If man is dead in sin, then God must elect to save him. These five points stand or fall together, bound in union by logical agreement. If a particular man is dead in trespasses and sin (T), only God alone unconditionally elects to save him (U). This same God only saves this particular man, whom he has chosen, by particular means, the death of Christ upon the cross for him (L). Only this God then draws this particular man to himself by grace, applying to him the redemption purchased by Christ for him (I). Finally, God only sovereignly keeps this particular man, whom he has saved, in the faith (P).

The doctrine of Limited Atonement states that the elect are the particular objects and the only beneficiaries of Christ's saving work on the cross. Christ's death upon the cross did not bring about potential or hypothetical salvation for all men without exception. It brought about actual salvation for a particular people, those whom God had chosen in Christ "before the foundation of the world" (Eph. 1:4).

The counter to Limited Atonement would be General or Universal Atonement, the idea that when Christ died upon the cross, he brought about the hypothetical or potential salvation of all men, conditioned upon their faith in him. Among the early Baptists in England, a distinction was made between Particular Baptists, who held to Limited (Particular) Atonement, and General Baptists, who held to General (Universal) Atonement.

Those early Particular Baptist were simply following a classic Protestant understand of the nature and extent of the atonement. Question 20 of the 1563 Heidelberg Catechism asks, "*Are all men then, as they perished in Adam, saved by Christ?*" To which, it answers: "No; only those who are ingrafted into Him, and receive all His benefits, by a true faith."[38] The first prooftext listed for this answer is from the angel of the Lord's announcement to Joseph at the conception of Jesus, "for he shall save his people from their sins" (Matt. 1:21). Christ came to save a particular people ("his people") from their sins. The second prooftext is Isaiah 53:11 in which the prophet declares that the Suffering Servant (Christ on the cross) "shall be satisfied," adding, "by his knowledge shall my righteous servant justify many; for he shall bear their iniquities." Notice the emphasis here on a Savior who is immediately "satisfied" by his suffering sacrifice. Notice also that his sacrifice does not justify all without exception but "many," as he bears "their iniquities." A robust doctrine of Limited Atonement undergirds this classic Protestant discipleship teaching, as it rejects not only "universalism," the idea that all men are saved whether they believe in Christ or not, but also the notion of "universal atonement," the idea that all men are hypothetically or potentially saved by Christ's death upon the cross.

---

[38] *The Heidelberg Catechism* (Grand Rapids, MI: Reformation Heritage Books, 2016), 8. A Baptistic revision of the Heidelberg Catechism was made by the English Particular Baptist pastor Hercules Collin in 1680 under the title *An Orthodox Catechism*. See Hercules Collins, *An Orthodox Catechism*, eds. Michael A. G. Haykin and G. Stephen Weaver, Jr. (Palmdale, CA: RBAP, 2014).

Observations on the Doctrine of Limited Atonement
We begin with nine observations on this doctrine:

(1) LIMITED ATONEMENT MAY BE BETTER REFERRED TO AS
"PARTICULAR REDEMPTION" OR "DEFINITE ATONEMENT."

The word "limited" may have some unintended negative connotations, as in "insufficient" or "inadequate." Yet this doctrine in no way implies any insufficiency in Christ's work on the cross. We may therefore choose to speak of particular redemption as opposed to general atonement or general redemption, which sees Christ's death as for all men but only applied on condition of human acceptance (linked to conditional election).

The term Limited Atonement is not meant to diminish the power of Christ's saving work on the cross. We sometimes attempt to capture this by affirming Christ's death on the cross was *sufficient* for all but *efficient* for the elect. It is not limited in its *power* (his death might have saved all if this had been God's design) but in its *extent* (God's purpose was that Christ's death would save many but not all). In fact, Charles Spurgeon argued that those who hold to universal atonement are actually the ones limiting the scope of Christ's atoning work:

> We are often told that we limit the atonement of Christ, because we say that Christ has not made a satisfaction for all men, or all would be saved. Now, our reply to this is, that, on the other hand, our opponents limit it: we do not. The Arminians say, Christ died for all men. Ask them what they mean by it. Did Christ die as to secure the salvation of all men? They say, "No, certainly not." We ask them the next question—Did Christ die so as to secure the salvation of any man in particular? They answer, "No. Christ has died that any man may be saved if"—

and then follow certain conditions of salvation. Now who is it that limits the death of Christ? Why, you. You say that Christ did not die so as infallibly to secure the salvation of anybody. We beg your pardon, when you say we limit Christ's death; we say, "No, my dear sir, it is you that do it." We say Christ so died that he infallibly secured the salvation of a multitude that no man can number, who through Christ's death not only may be saved, but are saved, must be saved and cannot by any possibility hazard of being anything but saved. You are welcome to your atonement; you may keep it. We will never renounce ours for the sake of it.[39]

The Bible speaks of a sense in which even the whole creation, which "groaneth and travaileth in pain," benefits from the reconciling work of Christ (Rom. 8:19–22), but this does not mean that all men profit from the saving benefit of Christ's death.

(2) LIMITED ATONEMENT, IN SOME FORM, IS HELD BY ALL BIBLE-AFFIRMING, EVANGELICAL BELIEVERS.

This statement is true in that faithful, evangelical Christians do not believe in the concept of universalism, that all people will be saved regardless of their beliefs and actions. Therefore, they necessarily believe that salvation is limited to those who are saved, who express repentance for sin and confess faith in Jesus Christ as Lord. As John 3:36 puts it: "He that believeth on the Son hath everlasting life: and he that believeth not the Son shall not see life; but the wrath of God abideth on him." To reject universalism, therefore, is necessarily to hold to some form of "limited" atonement.

---

[39] As quoted in J. I. Packer, "Introductory Essay" in John Owen, *The Death of Death in the Death of Christ* (Edinburgh/Carlisle, PA: Banner of Truth, 1959), 14, n. 1.

(3) Limited Atonement makes sense of the scriptural descriptions of redemption.

We begin with the Old Testament sacrifices. These sacrifices were made for specific persons and for a specific people. There were no universal atoning sacrifices in the Old Testament. Consider the description of the sacrifices on the Day of Atonement in Leviticus 16. Aaron was to make a sin offering, as an atonement "for himself, and for his house" and "for the people" and to confess over the scapegoat the sins "of the children of Israel" (Lev. 16: 11, 15, 21).

Next consider the "Suffering Servant" of Isaiah. In Isaiah 53:4–5 we read:

> Surely he hath borne our griefs, and carried our sorrows: yet we did esteem him stricken, smitten of God, and afflicted. But he was wounded for our transgressions, he was bruised for our iniquities: the chastisement for our peace was upon him, and with his stripes we are healed.

The prophet describes the particular sufferings of God's Servant for a specific people. He bears "our griefs" and carries "our sorrows." He was wounded for "our transgressions" and bruised for "our iniquities." The description is not of generic suffering or of hypothetical substitution. No, his suffering really accomplishes something for his people. In Isaiah 53:12, the prophet even states that "he bare the sin of many." Note the language of limitation. Not all will benefit, though "many" will.

Think also of the discriminating ministry of the Lord Jesus Christ, on behalf of his particular people, as recorded in the Gospels. Recall again that at his birth, the angel of the Lord heralds his conception to Joseph in Matthew 1:21 with these words: "And she shall bring forth a son, and thou shalt call His name JESUS: for he shall save his people from their sins." From the beginning, it is stated that he comes to redeem a particular people, *his* people. In full manhood, he declared to his disciples that "the Son of Man came not to be ministered unto, but to minister, and to give his life a ransom for many" (Matt. 20:28; cf. Mark 10:45). His saving work on the cross had a particular object—the redemption not of all without exception but of "many."

Limited Atonement is clearly stressed in John's Gospel. The Lord Jesus speaks of himself as the Good Shepherd who lays down his life for his sheep:

> I am the good shepherd, and know my sheep, and am known of mine. As the Father knoweth me, even so know I the Father: and I lay down my life for the sheep. And other sheep I have, which are not of this fold: them also I must bring, and they shall hear my voice; and there shall be one fold, and one shepherd. (John 10:14–16)

Notice that this good shepherd does not lay down his life for every sheep in the world without exception, but for the particular sheep which belong to his flock. When Jesus says, in verse 16, that he has other sheep, "which are not of this fold," he is not confirming universal redemption, but the fact that his sheep (disciples) includes both Jews and Gentiles. He even says to those who reject him, "But ye believe not, because ye are not of my sheep, as I said unto you" (John 10:26). In his high priestly prayer in John 17, the Lord Jesus limits his intercession exclusively to his own disciples: "I pray for them: I pray not for the world, but for them which thou hast given me: for they are thine" (John 17:9). His intercession, like his atoning work on the cross, is for a particular people.

In the ministry and writing of the apostle Paul one finds repeated emphasis on Christ's death as a "substitutionary atonement." He dies in the place of sinners and serves as a substitute for them. This concept is related to Limited Atonement in that it stresses that Christ's death on the cross was for a particular people. We begin this brief survey of Paul's thought in the book of Acts. In Luke's record of Paul's address to the Ephesian elders, Paul exhorted: "Take heed therefore unto yourselves, and to all the flock, over the which the Holy Ghost hath made you overseers, to feed the church of God, which he hath purchased with his own blood" (Acts 20:28). Notice that "the church of God" or body of believers, are those whom Christ "purchased with his own blood." He died not for all men without exception but for his church.

We turn next to Paul's New Testament letters. Remember that Paul wrote to distinct congregations and audiences. In Romans, Paul wrote to "all that be in Rome, beloved of God, called to be saints" (Rom. 1:7). He writes to believers in the church at Rome. Later, in Romans 5:8, he declares, "But God commendeth his love toward us, in that, while we were yet sinners, Christ died for us." Notice the first-person plural pronouns. Paul speaks here of the benefits that have come to believers, himself included, in the death of Christ. He does not say, "Christ died for all men without exception, so that some might possibly later come to believe." No, he declares, "Christ died for us." Paul emphasizes especially that Christ died for the sins of believers. There is no language of hypothetical redemption on behalf of unknown and undetermined recipients. Later, in Romans 8, Paul likewise declares that God the Father "spared not his own Son, but delivered him up for us all" (8:32). The "us all" for whom Christ died, are soon after plainly declared to be "God's elect" (8:33). The key for properly understanding Paul's words here is the fact that he, along with the other apostles, was not writing generic letters to all humanity but distinct letters to believers.

From Romans we can turn to 1 Corinthians, which is addressed, "to the church of God which is at Corinth" (1:2). In 1 Corinthians 8:11 Paul warns the saints not to offend a "weak brother" in the faith "for whom Christ died." He later describes the gospel he had preached at Corinth beginning with the affirmation, "that Christ died for our sins according to the Scriptures" (15:3).

Paul's letter to the Ephesians is addressed "to the saints which are at Ephesus, and to the faithful in Christ Jesus" (1:1). In Ephesians 1:7 he refers to Christ as the one "in whom we have redemption through his blood." In the Ephesian household code, Paul admonishes, 'Husbands, love your wives, even as Christ loved the church and gave himself for it" (5:25). Paul is certainly not encouraging Christian husbands indiscriminately to love and sacrifice themselves for all women without exception. He is urging Christian husbands to love and sacrifice themselves for their own particular wives. To clinch his point, Paul draws an analogy between the relationship of Christian husbands to their wives and Christ to his church. Just as Christ gave himself (on the cross) for a particular bride, for his church, so Christian husbands are to love and sacrifice themselves for their particular wives. This inspired analogy is rooted in the doctrine of Limited Atonement.

Paul is not the only apostle to teach Limited Atonement. We also find this teaching in the general epistles. Peter speaks of Christ as he "who his own self bare our sins in his body on the tree, that we, being dead to sins, should live unto righteousness: by whose stripes ye are healed" (1 Pet. 2:24). John says of Christ, that "he was manifested to take away our sins" (1 John 3:5). These letters also were written to believers in particular (cf. 1 Pet. 1:1-2; 1 John 1:1-4).

This brief survey has revealed that the doctrine of Limited Atonement is contained throughout the "all the counsel of God" in Holy Scripture (Acts 20:27). It is there in the Old Testament and especially in the New Testament, from the Gospels and Acts to the writings of Paul and the other apostles.

(4) LIMITED ATONEMENT MAKES SENSE OF SCRIPTURE'S AFFIRMATION THAT CHRIST HAS FULFILLED THE PLAN OF SALVATION.

The Scriptures speak boldly of Christ's death on the cross as having achieved the goal of God's plan of salvation. This has been done in reality and not merely hypothetically. Paul can speak of this plan having, "been hid in God, who created all things by Jesus Christ" (Eph. 3:9), but now it has been made manifest "according to the eternal purpose which he purposed in Christ Jesus our Lord" (Eph. 3:11). In his High Priestly Prayer, anticipating his crucifixion, Christ says to the Father, "I have finished the work which thou gavest me to do" (John 17:4). Just before his death on the cross, Christ does not say, "My work is almost finished, if men will only do their part to complete it." No! He says, "It is finished" (John 19:30).

We need to be clear that while Christ is a satisfied Savior, and the work of redemption on behalf of the elect has been fully achieved on the cross, it must also be applied to the hearts of believer as they receive the effectual calling and are justified by faith.[40] As Paul put it in the "golden chain of redemption," "Moreover whom he did predestinate, them he also called: and whom he called, them he also justified" (Rom. 8:30)

---

[40] See chapter 4 for a fuller explanation of effectual calling and the application of redemption.

(5) Limited atonement is required for an adequate
understanding of Substitutionary Atonement.

The doctrine of Limited Atonement unashamedly declares that the
Lord Jesus stood in the place of redeemed sinners. Thus, it affirms
the doctrine of the substitutionary atonement of Christ (i.e., that on
the cross the Lord Jesus stood in the place of redeemed sinners). In
John 15:13 Christ taught, "Greater love hath no man than this, that
a man lay down his life for his friends." That Christ's "friends" here is
a reference to his disciples is made clear by what Christ says next: "Ye
are my friends, if ye do whatsoever I command you" (John 15:14).
Compare the final greeting of the epistle of 3 John: "Greet the friends
by name" (1:14). As Paul says in Romans 5:6, "For when we were yet
without strength, in due time Christ died for the ungodly." Again, the
"we" here refers to believers. They are the ungodly ones who were set
free, because Christ stood in their place and took their penalty upon
himself. In 2 Corinthians 5:21 Paul states, "For he [God] hath made
him [Christ] to be sin for us, who knew no sin; that we might be
made the righteousness of God in him." Peter likewise affirms that on
the cross Christ "hath once suffered for sins, the just for the unjust"
(1 Peter 3:18). If Christ did not die on the cross for an actual people,
rather than merely for a hypothetical people, then the entire doctrine
of substitutionary atonement is completely undermined.

(6) Universal atonement makes salvation only a potential
possibility and not an assured reality.

The strength of the biblical argument for Limited Atonement is
accentuated all the more when one examines the weakness of the
counterargument for general or universal atonement, which can only
present Christ's death as a potential solution for man's sin. Consider
again, however, Isaiah's description of the suffering servant: "He shall

see of the travail of his soul, and shall be satisfied: by his knowledge shall my righteous servant justify many; for he shall bear their iniquity" (Isa. 53:11). In the New Testament, likewise, salvation is presented as an accomplished reality and not as a mere potentiality. In Galatians 3:13, Paul writes, "Christ hath redeemed us from the curse of the law, being made a curse for us: for it is written, Cursed is every one that hangeth on a tree." According to Paul, redemption had been fully accomplished in Christ's death on the cross. Limited Atonement affirms that Christ is a satisfied saviour. Christ did indeed fulfil the purpose for which he had been sent in his death on the cross and made certain the salvation of the elect.

The Christ of so-called "general redemption," however, must, of necessity, be an unsatisfied saviour. Theologian John Murray writes:

> Did Christ come to make the salvation of all men possible, to remove obstacles that stood in the way of salvation, and merely to make provision for salvation? Or did he come to save his people? Did he come to put all men in a salvable state? Or did he come to secure the salvation of all those ordained to eternal life? Did he come to make men redeemable? Or did he come effectually and infallibly to redeem? The doctrine of the atonement must be revised if, as atonement, it applies to those who finally perish as well as to those who are heirs of eternal life. In that event we should have to dilute the grand categories in terms of which the Scripture defines the atonement and deprive them of their most precious import and glory.[41]

Similarly, James Boice and Philip Ryken observe, "Christ's work on

---

[41] John Murray, *Redemption Accomplished and Applied* (Grand Rapids, MI: Eerdmans, 1955), 63–64.

the cross was not a hypothetical salvation for hypothetical believers, but a real and definite salvation for God's own chosen people."[42]

(7) UNIVERSAL ATONEMENT OPENS UP SOME UNSEEMLY POSSIBILITIES. We might add that the doctrine of supposed "general redemption" suggests some possibilities that are unseemly for biblical Christians to entertain. First, it would mean that there would be persons in hell for whom Christ died, but for whom Christ's death was insufficient to bring about their salvation. Likewise, it opens the possibility of "double payment" suggesting that Christ could bear the wrath of God on the cross for a person's sin, but then that person could reject Christ and suffer God's wrath for those same sins. If Christ truly bore the wrath of God for a person's sin on the cross, how then could such a person still have to suffer damnation for that sin?

General redemption also opens up the hypothetical possibility that *no one* would be saved by Christ's death on the cross. This would mean that Christ's death on the cross would *potentially* have been for no redeeming purpose. Such a circumstance would empty the cross of its meaning. The doctrine of Limited Atonement excludes this absurdity.

(8) UNIVERSAL ATONEMENT HAS HISTORICALLY LED TO A DRIFT TOWARD THEOLOGICAL LIBERALISM AND UNIVERSALISM. One can sadly trace the drift of many denominations which have rejected particular redemption while drifting in the direction of liberalism and universalism. The typical historical pattern has been, first, to jettison the sovereignty of God in salvation; second, to embrace a man-centred view of salvation; and, finally, to embrace universalism.

---

[42] James Montgomery Boice and Philip Graham Ryken, *The Doctrines of Grace* (Wheaton, IL: Crossway, 2002), 123.

This was the fate of many of the General Baptists of England, so called for their embrace of "general" atonement, who eventually abandoned orthodoxy and became unitarian.[43] Many of the historic Congregationalist churches of New England followed this trend toward doctrinal declension. In the days of Jonathan Edwards and the Great Awakening, they were staunch evangelical Calvinists. Over time many of these churches first embraced Arminianism, then liberalism, and, ultimately, they became Unitarians and Universalists.[44] Those who are squeamish in affirming the particular benefits of Christ's redeeming work have a tendency to be squeamish about teaching doctrines such as the damnation of the wicked, hell, and eternal suffering. We should take note of the fact that no theologically liberal denomination has ever consistently held to Limited Atonement.

(9) LIMITED ATONEMENT SHOULD BE HELD WITH HUMILITY AND CARE. This doctrine speaks to a conviction about the witness of Scripture as to the meaning and extent of the atonement. We should remember that God alone knows the identity of those for whom Christ died. As with election, we do not know their identity. Firmly holding to the doctrine of Limited Atonement, however, should give us boldness in preaching the gospel. The gospel is to be preached freely and without distinction to all men. We know there are those out there for whom

---

[43] See H. Leon McBeth, *The Baptist Heritage* (Nashville, TN: B&H, 1987), 154–56.

[44] According to the website of the Unitarian Universalist Association of Congregations (uua. org), the Universalists organized in 1793 and the Unitarians in 1825. They consolidated in 1961. It states: "Both groups trace their roots in North America to the early Massachusetts settlers and to the founders of the Republic." Indeed, they sprang from once fiercely orthodox congregations. The description of the organization's beliefs sounds in many ways like what one might hear from Arminians, moderate Baptists, mainline Protestants, and even some broad evangelicals in our day: "Unitarian Universalism is a liberal religion with Jewish-Christian roots. It has no creed. It affirms the worth of human beings, advocates freedom of belief and the search for advancing truth, and tries to provide a warm, open, supportive community for people who believe that ethical living is the supreme witness of religion."

Christ died. Such persons will recognize their Shepherd's voice when they hear it (John 10:27). When Christ is lifted up, he will be pleased to draw all who are his own to himself (John 12:32).

Objection passages

Many of the objections raised against the doctrine of Limited Atonement relate to the interpretation of various passages using the word "all." Those who object usually take for granted that the word "all" in every instance refers to "all humanity." When read in context, however, the word "all" very often refers not to "all human beings without exception" but to "all the elect."

We make this kind of verbal discernment in everyday discourse. One might, for example, read or hear a report like the following on the news: "There was an accident in the city involving a single vehicle with four passengers. All were killed." Upon listening to this report, one does not suppose that all human beings were killed or that all the people in the city were killed in the accident. The context makes clear that "all" refers to all four of the passengers. Context is a key to right interpretation. Many read the Gospels and the epistles as universal missives to all humanity, without exception, rather than as communication written to particular Christian audiences. This clouds their ability rightly to understand these passages.

Many also misunderstand the astonishment expressed in the New Testament over the fact that both Jews and Gentiles (all kinds of men; men from the whole world) are being saved. Paul, for example, is staggered with amazement that in Christ "the Gentiles should be fellowheirs, and of the same body, and partakers of his promise in Christ by the gospel" (Eph. 3:6). Some confuse this emphasis on the fact that *all sorts* of men (Jew and Gentile, slave and free, men and women) have been redeemed with the notion that *all men* are redeemed (universalism) or potentially redeemed (Arminianism). Although Christ's work on the cross does extend to all kinds of men, all men, without exception, are not saved!

Here are a few examples of "objection passages" offered as supposed "defeaters" to the doctrine of Limited Atonement, along with some responses suggesting a proper interpretation of these passages:

◆ The next day John seeth Jesus coming unto him, and saith, Behold the Lamb of God, which taketh away the sin of the world. (John 1:29)

Interpretation: Yes, Jesus takes away the sin of the world. He reverses the impact of the fall and begins to roll back the clock to pre-fall perfection, a process that will only be fully accomplished at his second coming with the arrival of the new heaven and the new earth (Rev. 21:1). The sins of all unregenerate men, however, clearly are not removed. God's wrath still remains on unbelievers (John 3:36).

◆ For God so loved the world, that he gave his only begotten Son, that whosoever believeth in him should not perish, but have everlasting life. (John 3:16)

Interpretation: This verse is sometimes presented as if it is some kind of astounding refutation of the doctrine of Limited Atonement, a veritable "silver bullet" against five-point Calvinism. It is, in fact, nothing of the sort. God's love for the world does not mean universal salvation (i.e., that all men, without exception, are saved), nor does this verse even directly address the extent of the atonement. Rather, it speaks to the depth of God's love in sending his Son to be incarnate among men (John 1:14).

The Lord Jesus almost immediately afterwards makes clear that the world was in darkness: "men loved darkness rather than light, because their deeds were evil" (John 3:19). He also speaks in John 9:39 of the judgement he has come to bring, "For judgment I am come into this world, that they which see not might see, and that they which see might be made blind." If unregenerate men come to believe in Christ, it is only by the grace of God (see Eph. 2:8–9). The new birth comes "not of blood, nor of the will of the flesh, nor of the will of man, but of God" (John 1:13). The central point of John 3:16 is that salvation comes from God's love alone.

John 3:16 also stresses the universal scope of salvation. John later records that when Christ entered Jerusalem the Pharisees observed, "behold, the world is gone after him" (John 12:19). They apparently did so because they observed that "certain Greeks . . . that came up to worship at the feast" (John 12:20) were present among Christ's followers. These Greeks say to Philip, "Sir, we would see Jesus" (12:21). The context does not make clear whether these "certain Greeks" were Hellenistic, Greek-speaking Jews of the diaspora or Gentile "God-fearers" who had been drawn to worship the God of the Old Testament. Perhaps it included both. The point being stressed is that all kinds of men were being drawn to Christ. The emphasis in John 3:16, expressed throughout the Fourth Gospel, is that God's purpose in sending Christ is to save men from the whole world.

John 3:16, then, can only properly be understood within the context of the rest of Christ's teachings as recorded in the Gospel of John. When thus examined, it does not contradict the doctrine of Limited Atonement.

◆ For the love of Christ constraineth us; because we thus judge, that if one died for all, then were all dead: and that he died for all, that they which live should not henceforth live unto themselves, but unto him which died for them, and rose again. (2 Cor. 5:14–15)

Interpretation: Paul's focus here is on elect believers, those who are part of the new creation. This epistle is directed "unto the church of God which is at Corinth" (2 Cor. 1:1). Christ died for all the elect, while they were still dead in their trespasses and sins. The elect, who have been saved by God's grace, are now those who no longer live for themselves but only for Christ.

◈ I exhort, therefore, that, first of all, supplications, prayers, intercessions, and giving of thanks, be made for all men; For kings, and for all that are in authority; that we may lead a quiet and peaceable life in all godliness and honesty. For this is good and acceptable in the sight of God our Savior; Who will have all men to be saved, and to come unto the knowledge of the truth. For there is one God, and one mediator between God and men, the man Christ Jesus; who gave himself a ransom for all, to be testified, in due time. Whereunto I am ordained a preacher, and an apostle, (I speak the truth in Christ and lie not;) a teacher of the Gentiles in faith and verity. (1 Tim. 2:1–7)

Interpretation: To understand this passage, one must first consider the context. Paul is exhorting Timothy concerning prayer. Prayer is to be made "for all men [Greek: *hyper pantōn anthrōpōn*]" without exception. This includes both pagan, Gentile rulers ("for kings, and for all that are in authority"), as well as for believers ("that we may lead a quiet and peaceable life in all godliness and honesty").

The interpretive problem arises in verse 4, when Paul says that God desires "all men [Greek: *pantas anthrōpous*] to be saved." What does Paul mean by "all men"? Is he suggesting, as Arminians claim, that all men without exception might possibly be saved and that this is the will of God? If this is God's will and if God is sovereign, however, this would mean that Paul is advocating universalism (all men are saved without exception). This cannot be Paul's intention.

There are at least two plausible explanations for Paul's words here that are consistent with his teaching elsewhere. First, the phrase "all men" in verse 4 might be taken as referring to all kinds of men, both Jews and Gentiles, much as the term is used in verse 1.

Second, Paul might have had in mind a distinction between God's revealed will and his decretive or "secret" will. God's revealed will is indeed that all men without exception would be saved. He is a good and loving God who does not take pleasure in the death of the wicked (cf. Ezek. 18:23; 33:11). His decretive (decreed) or "secret" will, however, must be that all men will not, in fact, be saved. Certainly, if God in his sovereignty desired the salvation of every single human being he could accomplish it. This clearly is not what is meant here, since so many passages (John 3:36 among them) remind us that all will not, in fact, be saved.

◆ For therefore we both labour and suffer reproach, because we trust in the living God, who is the Saviour of all men, specially of those that believe. (1 Tim. 4:10)

Interpretation: The question here is what did Paul mean when he referred to the Lord Jesus Christ as "the Saviour of all men, specially of those that believe"? Is Paul saying that Christ is the hypothetical "Saviour of all men" and that this salvation is only actualized by those who believe when they trust in Christ? If so, then it would seem to promote universal redemption and undermine particular redemption.

To understand Paul's meaning, however, one must first examine the context of these words. Paul is writing to encourage the young minister Timothy, urging him to remember that in the midst of difficult labours and the suffering of reproach, he should trust in the living God. Paul is not, in fact, addressing here the doctrine of salvation but the doctrine of providence. He refers to the Lord as "the Saviour (Greek: *Sōtēr*) of all men." The term "Saviour" can indeed can be used to refer to the God of the Bible and specifically to the Lord Jesus Christ as a Redeemer. It can also, however, be used to refer to God as a Provider. The Romans could refer to their emperors as "saviours," not meaning that they provided spiritual salvation, but material protection. Taken in this manner, to call God "the Saviour of all men" would be parallel to Christ's teaching in Matthew 5:45 that God causes the rain to fall and the sun to shine on both the just and the unjust.

In his commentary on this verse, John Calvin argues that the main point is that believers lose nothing of God's providence when they are tried by adversity. He thus takes "Saviour" here as "a general term" denoting "one who defends and preserves."[45] He concludes that Paul's meaning is "that the kindness of God extends to all men." If God's goodness and care extends to all men, then, "how much more is it experienced by the godly, who hope in him?"

The Puritan commentator Matthew Poole, likewise, takes "Saviour" as used here to mean, "The Preserver of all man, the Preserver

---

[45] John Calvin, *Calvin's Commentaries*, Calvin Translation Society, vol. 21, (Grand Rapids, MI: Baker Books, 2009), 112.

of man and beast."[46] He compares this verse to Psalm 33:18–19, where one finds a similar stress on God's preservation of his people. Poole adds:

> This seemeth rather to be the sense of the text, than to understand it of eternal salvation, for so God is not the actual Saviour of all; besides that the text seemeth to speak of a work proper to the Father, rather than to the Son.

Poole raises a major issue with the Arminian interpretation. If "the Saviour of all men" is taken as a reference to general atonement, it lends support to the unsavoury notion of universal salvation, a concept clearly counter to the biblical witness (cf. John 3:36).

So, 1 Timothy 4:10 does not contradict the doctrines of grace. When Scripture is "rightly divided" it must be interpreted as a testimony to God's special care for his people. If the Lord provides for all men, will he not, all the more, provide for his own dear people?

This is precisely the way in which the Particular Baptists of the seventeenth century understood this verse. It is cited as the first prooftext in support of the section "Of Divine Providence," of the Second London [Baptist] Confession, which reads: "As the providence of God doth in general reach to all creatures, so after a most special manner it taketh care of His church, and disposeth all things to the good thereof." (2LCF 5.7)

◆ But we see Jesus, who was made a little lower than the angels for the suffering of death, crowned with glory and honour;

---

[46] Matthew Poole, *A Commentary on the Holy Bible*, vol. 3 (Peabody, MA: Hendrickson, 2010), 783. Note: Though the entire work is attributed to Poole as author, much of it was completed by others after his death.

that he by the grace of God should taste death for every man. (Heb. 2:9)

Interpretation: The question here is what the author of Hebrews meant when he said that Christ tasted death "for every man." Did he mean, as Arminians suggest, that Christ died for the hypothetical salvation of every man? If this is the case, his death did not accomplish actual salvation for any particular man. Or, it might be asked, did the author of Hebrews mean that in tasting death Christ accomplished actual salvation for absolutely every man without exception? If this is the case, then every man is saved by Christ's death, and the author of Hebrews was teaching universalism, in contrast to all other teaching in the New Testament.

What alternatives are left for us to consider? There are two much better interpretive possibilities. First, when the author of Hebrews said that Christ tasted death for every man, he might have meant that Christ died on the cross for every kind of man, Jew and Gentile, slave and free, men and women. Second, he might have meant that Christ tasted death for every man who is among the elect of God. Both of these interpretations are more reasonable, and they are completely consistent with the doctrine of Limited Atonement.

◆ But there were false prophets also among the people, even as there shall be false teachers among you, who privily shall bring in damnable heresies, even denying the Lord that bought them, and bring upon themselves swift destruction. (2 Pet. 2:1)

Interpretation: Arminians might argue that this verse suggests there are unsaved persons whom Christ "bought" (i.e., for whom he died, offering the possibility of their salvation). We respond by noting that

Peter's point here is that there will be false prophets and false professors of faith among God's people even as there were in days of old. Peter offers a parody of such persons' false claims to be in Christ. They claim to be among the blood-bought saints, but their heretical teaching exposes the falsehood of that claim. When they espouse "damnable heresies" they expose their false faith, denying the Lord they claim has bought them.

When the Puritan John Owen examined this text in *The Death of Death in the Death of Christ,* he made the following key observations:

a) The word for "Lord" here is not *kurios,* the name that believers give to the Lord Jesus, but *despotes,* Master. This implies that these men knew Jesus Christ to be powerful, but they did not know him as their Lord.

b) When Peter spoke of them being "bought" or "redeemed" he might have been using that word in a way that did not imply salvation. These false prophets had benefited from the teaching of Christ, perhaps by being removed from the legalism of the Jews or the paganism of the Gentiles, but they were not savingly redeemed by the blood of Christ.

c) Peter's point here is that, in the estimation of others, they were believed to be saved. They seemed to be among the redeemed. Owen concludes, however, they were in truth "saints in show— really wolves and hypocrites, of old ordained to condemnation."[47]

 ◆ The Lord is not slack concerning his promise, as some men count slackness; but is longsuffering to us-ward, not willing that any should perish but that all should come to repentance. (2 Pet. 3:9)

[47] John Owen, *The Death of Death in the Death of Christ*, 250–252.

Interpretation: This passage obviously does not mean that God intends to save everyone (universalism). The only proper way to understand Peter's words here is to conclude he is saying that God is not willing *that any of the elect* should perish but that *all the elect* should be saved.

⬥ And he is the propitiation for our sins: and not for ours only, but also for the sins of the whole world. (1 John 2:2)

Interpretation: In context, John is most likely referring to the fact that the saving benefits of Christ's death applied both to Jewish Christians, like himself, and to Gentile Christians, people from every nation, tribe, and tongue. The wonder of Jewish believers like John and Paul is that men and women from "the whole world" had been included in God's plan of redemption through Christ. In Ephesians, Paul can speak of the inclusion of Gentiles as "the mystery of Christ", which "in other ages was not made known unto the sons of men, as it is now revealed unto his holy apostles and prophets by the Spirit", namely, "That the Gentiles should be fellowheirs, and of the same body, and partakers of the promise in Christ by the gospel" (Eph. 3:4–6; cf. Col. 1:26–27). John here wonders at the same reality.

Conclusion

The doctrine of Limited Atonement makes the best sense of the total scriptural witness to Christ's saving work on the cross. Some will protest that embracing this doctrine will kill evangelism. They suggest that the Christian preacher must proclaim to all without exception: "Christ died for you." One cannot find an example of this kind of evangelistic appeal, however, in the New Testament. We should proclaim instead, as Spurgeon suggested, "You are a sinner and Jesus died for sinners. If you would be saved, you must repent of your sin and believe the gospel."[48] J. I. Packer likewise affirms:

> The fact is that the NT never calls on any man to repent on the ground that Christ died specifically and particularly for him. The basis on which the NT invites sinners to put faith in Christ is simply that they need Him, and that he offers Himself to them, and that those who receive Him are promised all the benefits that His death secured for His people. What is universal and all-inclusive in the NT is the invitation to faith, and the promise of salvation to all who believe . . . . The gospel is not 'believe that Christ died for everybody's sins, and therefore yours,' any more than it is, 'believe that Christ died only for certain people's sins, and so perhaps not for yours.' The gospel is, 'believe on the Lord Jesus Christ, who died for sins, and now offers you Himself as your Saviour.' This is the message which we are to take to the world. We have no business to ask them to put faith in any view of the extent of the atonement; our job is to point them to the living Christ, and summon them to trust in Him.[49]

The doctrine of Limited Atonement stresses the final, complete, and total success of Christ's work in redeeming his people. As the writer of Hebrews so boldly put it: "But this man, after he had offered one sacrifice for sins for ever, sat down on the right hand of God" (10:12). One is seated when his work is completed, final. Christ is a satisfied Savior, knowing he has accomplished what he set out to do. This is the message that gives the church boldness in its preaching of the cross.

---

[48] As quoted in Boice and Ryken, *Doctrines of Grace*, 133.
[49] J. I. Packer, *Evangelism and the Sovereignty of God* (Downers Grove, IL: IVP, 1961), 68–69.

Chapter 4
IRRESISTIBLE GRACE

I rresistible grace describes the way God graciously redeems those purchased by Christ. Grace is applied to the saved in such a way that their hearts and lives are utterly and gladly taken captive to Christ. The redeemed are drawn by God's Spirit to trust completely in Christ for their salvation. God lovingly overcomes any stubborn resistance within the elect and makes the redeemed his glad and willing servants. To say that this is "irresistible grace" is first to say that it is an act of God's grace toward the redeemed sinner, and, second, that it cannot be resisted or confounded by any power within or without the man who is the object of God's saving purpose.

We have already discussed man's state in sin and his total inability to seek God (T); God's plan to save mankind and his sovereign election of those who would be saved (U); and God's accomplishment of redemption through Christ's death on the cross (L). We now come to the application of that redemption to the hearts of sinful men so that through faith in Christ they are saved (the I of TULIP).

At this point, the doctrines of grace demonstrate a robust trinitarian theology: the Father elects; the Son redeems; the Spirit applies redemption. The doctrine of Irresistible Grace stresses that salvation comes about, in particular, as a work of the Holy Spirit. Christ told Nicodemus that one must be "born of the Spirit" to enter the kingdom of God (c.f. John 3:5–8).

Imagine the following scenario: Two people hear the gospel

preached. One is converted and becomes a solid believer. The other is left cold by the gospel and remains in his unbelief. What made the difference in the response of the two men? The Arminian says the difference rests completely in the decisions made by the two men: the first man chose God, and the second man did not. The Arminian implies that there was some special quality within, or some work performed by the first man that distinguished him in the eyes of God from the second man. The doctrines of grace, however, say that both men would have remained in an unregenerate state and indifferent to the gospel, if the Holy Spirit had not worked to quicken and bring about faith. They would contend that the first man, like anyone who experiences conversion, was saved by a sovereign act of God's free grace alone. The first man in this illustration would have been just as indifferent to the gospel as the second man if the Spirit of God had not graciously drawn him to Christ.

Though we have rightly noted the role of the Holy Spirit in the application of redemption, as we shall see below, the Bible can also speak of the Father drawing men to salvation and the Son savingly revealing himself to sinners. Salvation is indeed a work of the triune God.

Basic Scriptural Background

To understand the doctrine of God's irresistible grace, we must first examine the biblical teaching on this subject. The Gospels record that the Lord Jesus himself taught that the only way a person would come to believe in him was through divine intervention. In Matthew 11:27 Jesus said, "All things are delivered unto me of my Father: and no man knoweth the Son, but the Father; neither knoweth any man the Father, save the Son, and he to whomsoever the Son will reveal him" (cf. Luke 10:22). Not only does the Lord Jesus make clear that no one can know God except by knowing him (cf. John 14:6), but he also stresses that only those whom he *wills* have this truth revealed to them. When Scriptures stress the role of "free will" in salvation, the emphasis is not on the "free will" of human beings but of God Himself (cf. John 1:13; Rom. 9:15–16).

When asked by his disciples why he taught in parables, Christ replied, "Because it is given unto you to know the mysteries of the kingdom of heaven, but to them it is not given" (Matt. 13:11). He continued: "For whosoever hath, to him shall be given, and he shall have abundance: but whosoever hath not, from him shall be taken away even that he hath. Therefore speak I to them in parables: because they seeing see not; and hearing they hear not, neither do they understand" (13:12–13). The Lord Jesus did not tell parables to make the gospel clearer to outsiders, to "put the cookie on the bottom shelf." Quite the opposite! He spoke in parables so that only his sincere disciples would understand. Those who come to understand and trust Christ do so because God has willed to give them understanding.

The Gospel of John contains perhaps more emphasis on the doctrine of Irresistible Grace than anywhere else in the Bible. In John 5:21, Jesus says, "For as the Father raiseth up the dead, and quickeneth them, even so the Son quickeneth whom he will." As in Matthew 11:27 and Luke 10:22, the apostle John stresses in his Gospel that Christ taught that those who believe in him are given to him by the Father:

All that the Father giveth me shall come to me; and him that cometh to me I will in no wise cast out. (John 6:37)

No man can come to me, except the Father which hath sent me draw him: and I will raise him up at the last day. (John 6:44)

And he said, Therefore said I unto you, that no man can come unto me, except it were given unto him of my Father. (John 6:65)

We should take special note of John 6:44 and its use of the language of divine "drawing." The Greek verb here is *elkuō*. The same verb appears in John 12:32 when Christ says, "And I, if I be lifted up from the earth, will draw all men unto me." Unless one wants to affirm universalism (the idea that all people are eventually saved regardless of their response to Christ), the "all men" in John 12:32 should be taken as a reference to the fact that all kinds of people (i.e., Jews and Gentiles, slave and free, male and female; cf. Gal. 3:28) will be drawn to him. As previously noted in this study, biblical faith affirm the *universality* of the gospel but not *universalism*. The point here is that God supernaturally draws those from all backgrounds to be saved in Christ.

It is also helpful to look at other examples of the use of this verb *elkuō* in the New Testament. In John 18:10 it is used in reference to Peter drawing his sword. In John 21:6, 11 it is used in reference to the disciples dragging a net full of fish. In Acts 16:19 and 21:30 it is used in reference to Paul being dragged away by the authorities. Finally, in James 2:6 it is used in reference to the rich dragging the poor into court. God the Father must draw or drag the unbeliever to Christ in the way a sword is drawn from its sheath (the sword does not decide to unsheathe itself!), in the way fishermen carry their nets to shore, and in the way someone with power and authority compels another to come to court.

This same stress on God's irresistible grace can, of course, also be found in the letters of Paul. Multiple examples from Paul will appear below, but for now we will mention Philippians 1:29 where

Paul writes, "For unto you it is given in the behalf of Christ, not only to believe on him, but also to suffer for his sake". Note the passive verb here: "unto you it is given." The notion expressed here of God granting belief in (and suffering for) Christ perfectly parallels Christ's own words in John 6:65 that no man can come to Him unless it is given to him by the Father. God is the one who gives, initiates, bestows, draws, regenerates, and pursues. To Him is due all the glory for salvation from beginning to end.

Observations on the Doctrine of Irresistible Grace

Having covered some of the basic biblical foundations for the doctrine of irresistible grace, we will now offer five key observations on this doctrine:

(1) IRRESISTIBLE GRACE IS BASED ON A RADICAL BIBLICAL UNDERSTANDING OF GOD'S FREE GRACE.

This doctrine stresses biblical grace as completely unmerited favour. It is truly a free gift of God. Even the best of human deeds are like filthy rags before God (see Isa. 64:6). Salvation is not a result of human works; it is an act of God's free grace alone. In Romans 4, Paul provides a faithful interpretation of the significance of the way in which the salvation of Father Abraham is described in Scripture, "Abraham believed God, and it was counted unto him for righteousness" (Rom. 4:3; cf. Gen. 15:6). Paul then explains, "But to him that worketh not, but believeth on him that justifieth the ungodly, his faith is counted for righteousness, Even as David also describeth the blessedness of the man, unto whom God imputeth righteousness without works" (Rom. 4:5–6). Abraham did not have to do any work to gain a right standing with God. Even his faith was not a work. Even his faith came by God's grace.

In what might be called the *Magna Carta* of the gospel, Paul proclaims in Ephesians 2:8–9: "For by grace are ye saved through faith; and that not of yourselves: it is the gift of God: not of works, lest any man should boast." Likewise, in 2 Timothy 1:9 Paul urges believers not to be ashamed of the gospel that has come by the power of God "Who hath saved us, and called us with an holy calling, not according to our works, but according to his own purpose and grace, which was given us in Christ Jesus before the world began". Note the passive verb at the close of this verse: God's grace "was given us." Duane Edward Spencer states, "We are not saved because he foreknew of a *good work of faith* resulting from *our* positive volition toward Jesus. No, that would put God in debt to sinful man. Paul says it was 'all of grace.' Hallelujah!"[50] The doctrine of Irresistible Grace is built on the Scriptural affirmation that God's saving grace is radically free.

(2) IRRESISTIBLE GRACE IS BASED ON THE SOVEREIGNTY OF GOD'S FREE WILL.

Perhaps the central theme of the entire Bible is the greatness and sovereignty of God. His will and his purposes are being worked out on earth, and he is sovereign over all that transpires in his creation. Solomon declared that even the most powerful people of earth merely do his bidding: "The king's heart is in the hand of the LORD, as the rivers of water: he turneth it whithersover he will" (Prov. 21:1). The Bible affirms in no uncertain terms the absolute sovereignty of God.

Salvation, in particular, is consistently traced back to the exercise of God's sovereign will. John affirms this in his prologue to the Fourth Gospel. He describes Christ as the "true Light" that came into the world, although "the world knew him not" (John 1:9–10). He continues: "But

---

[50] Duane Edward Spencer, *TULIP: The Five Points of Calvinism in the Light of Scripture* (Grand Rapids, MI: Baker Books, 1979), 59.

as many as received him, to them gave he power to become the sons of God, even to them that believe on his name" (1:12). If we were to stop at this verse, we might have a question about the order of salvation. Do believers first receive Christ and then God grants them power? Or does God grant them power and then they are able to receive Christ? The answer is made clear in John 1:13 which describes believers as those "Which were born, not of blood, nor of the will of the flesh, nor of the will of man, but of God." Clearly, the life-giving power of God which brings about conversion must first be given before a man can believe in Christ. God alone is the author of salvation.

God's will in salvation is seen in the classic description of redemption in the first chapter of Paul's epistle to the Ephesians. The apostle begins by stressing the doctrine of election, saying that God "hath chosen us in him before the foundation of the world" (Eph. 1:4). This predestination to adoption as God's children came about "according to the good pleasure of his will" (1:5). The stress here is clearly on the divine will, not human free will. Paul says God works "according to the good pleasure of his will" rather than "contingent upon the free will choices of sinful men." This theme continues when Paul says that God has "made known to us the mystery of his will, according to his good pleasure, which he hath purposed in himself" (1:9). The point here is the mystery of the revelation of the divine will, not the mystery of his foreknowledge of human free will choices!

If any reader is unclear as to Paul's intentions, the theme is repeated in the verses that follow, as Paul affirms that in Christ "we have obtained an inheritance, being predestinated according to the purpose of him who worketh all things after the counsel of his will" (1:11). There is no suggestion in this chapter that God's work of salvation is in any way contingent upon the supposed free will choices of sinful men! This was a crucial point in our previous discussion of

Unconditional Election, but it is also relevant to our understanding of Irresistible Grace. God saves those whom he sovereignly chooses, and he employs sovereign means to overcome any resistance to his saving purposes.

(3) IRRESISTIBLE GRACE IS BASED ON THE BIBLICAL UNDERSTANDING THAT, APART FROM GOD'S SAVING GRACE, MAN'S WILL IS TOTALLY ENSLAVED TO SIN AND TO SATAN.

We noted above the vital connection between the doctrines of Irresistible Grace and Unconditional Election. God's election does not consist of God ratifying by his foreknowledge man's free will choice of God. Apart from God's grace, no man will ever exercise his will to choose the gospel. God's will must overcome man's fallen will. The doctrine of Irresistible Grace is therefore vitally related to the doctrine of Total Depravity. An unregenerate man will not choose Christ apart from God's direct and purposeful intervention. All men are hell-bound. God, by his grace and for his glory, saves some.

Sometimes opponents of Irresistible Grace point to the Lord Jesus's words in Matthew 23:37 as a supposed refutation of this doctrine: "O Jerusalem, Jerusalem, thou that killest the prophets, and stonest them which are sent unto thee, how often would I have gathered thy children together, even as a hen gathereth her chickens under her wings, and ye would not!" (cf. Luke 13:34). The final phrase of this verse "and ye would not!" is rendered in the New King James Version, "but you were not willing!" When rightly understood, however, rather than contradicting the need for God's irresistible grace, these words prove the point! There is no denying that man has free will. The problem is that man's will is corrupted. The Lord Jesus stretches out open arms, as it were, but unregenerate men are not willing to come to him. They will not do so until and unless God himself changes their hearts. They are by nature "dead in trespasses and sins" (Eph. 2:1), "the children of disobedience" (2:2), and "the children of wrath" (2:3), until God makes them alive in Christ (2:5). The Lord must overcome, even overwhelm, their unwillingness to come to him and draw them to himself.

The Bible further teaches that man's will, in its unregenerate state, is not only corrupted and enslaved by his own sin, but it is also under the sway of the malevolent will of the devil, also referred to as Satan. The Lord Jesus upbraided his unregenerate Jewish opponents, "Ye are of your father the devil, and the lusts of your father ye will do" (John 8:44). Note how jarring his words are. He does not say, "You are basically good people. You are all my children. Please listen to me and choose to believe in me so I can save you!" He says that unregenerate men are in the clutches of the evil one.

It has been said that God is a first-rate power; Satan is a second-rate power; and man is a third-rate power.[51] The unregenerate have been taken captive to do Satan's will. This is made clear in Paul's admonition to Timothy urging him to correct his unconverted opponents: "if God peradventure will give them repentance to the acknowledgement of the truth; And that they may recover themselves out of the snare of the devil, who are taken captive by him at his will" (2 Tim. 2:25–26). God's irresistible grace is needed not only to overcome man's own sin, but also to remove sinners from the grip of Satan's powerful will.

(4) IRRESISTIBLE GRACE RESTS ON THE UNDERSTANDING THAT
REGENERATION PRECEDES FAITH.

In regeneration the human heart and will are transformed. This is the new birth or being born "from above." Regeneration must precede faith. The Lord Jesus said to Nicodemus, "Verily, verily, I say unto

---

[51] Spencer, *TULIP*, 58.

thee, Except a man be born again, he cannot see the kingdom of God" (John 3:3). Luke describes the conversion or spiritual change that occurred in Lydia at Philippi which enabled her to grasp Paul's preaching of the gospel in this way: "whose heart the Lord opened that she attended unto the things which were spoken by Paul" (Acts 16:14). Paul likewise describes the common salvation experienced by believers in Titus 3:5: "Not by works of righteousness which we have done, but according to his mercy he saved us, by the washing of regeneration, and renewing [Greek: *anakainosis*; literally 'making new again'] of the Holy Ghost."

The Christian is one who has been made a new man spiritually, having "put on the new man, who is renewed in knowledge after the image of him that created him" (Col. 3:10). The man who is in Christ is "a new creature: old things are passed away; behold, all things are become new" (2 Cor. 5:17). The present spiritual life of believers is immediately transformed, and at the resurrection believers will fully bear the image of Christ, which is the image of God renewed in them, as their spirits are united with their resurrection bodies, and sin is completely overcome in them: "And as we have borne the image of the earthy, we shall also bear the image of the heavenly" (1 Cor. 15:49). Just as man is incapable of bringing about his own final resurrection, so he is incapable of bringing about his regeneration. This comes from God alone.

(5) Irresistible Grace does not suggest that any are saved or rejected "against their will".

The word "irresistible" in Irresistible Grace stresses the fact that God's purposes of grace cannot be thwarted. God's purposes will prevail in the end. God's will cannot be resisted. To avoid any confusion, some prefer to speak of God's "efficacious grace," or "effectual grace."

Two arguments are sometimes put forward as straw-men against the doctrine of Irresistible Grace. First, some suggest that this teaching indicates that God "forces" some men to believe in Christ, contrary to their desires. They might even make it sound as if this doctrine suggests that the Lord drags the elect kicking and screaming into the arms of Jesus! Second, some suggest that the doctrines of grace teach that there are some men who want to believe in Jesus, but who are rejected because they are not among the elect.

Let us attempt to answer these objections. First, no one is saved "against his will." Once the heart is regenerated, renewed, and transformed by God's grace the converted man wants to know of Christ. No one has to force him to love Christ. The idea of forcing a regenerate man to love Christ would be like forcing a typical child to go to an amusement park or to eat ice cream!

Second, the reprobate do not want to believe in Christ. The hypothetical person who wants to believe in Christ but who is rejected by God does not exist! The apostle Paul taught, "For whosoever shall call upon the name of the Lord shall be saved" (Rom. 10:13). Paul drew this quotation from the Old Testament prophet Joel: "And it shall come to pass, that whosoever shall call on the name of the LORD shall be delivered: for in Mount Zion and in Jerusalem shall be deliverance, as the LORD hath said, and in the remnant whom the LORD shall call" (Joel 2:32). Joel's point is that all those who call on the name of the Lord are those who have been effectually called (regenerated) by the Lord! Apart from God's effectual call and regeneration, no man wants to believe in Christ. There are no unregenerate men who desire Christ.

Conclusion

The evangelical minister Harry Ironside once told a story of an older Christian who gave his testimony. "He told how God had sought him out and found him, how God had loved him, called him, saved him, delivered him, cleansed him, and healed him—a great witness to the grace, power, and glory of God." After the meeting a man took him aside and said, "I appreciated all you said about what God did for you. But you didn't mention anything about your part in it. Salvation is really part us and part God. You should have mentioned something about your part." "'Oh yes,' the older Christian said, 'I apologize for that. I really should have said something about my part. My part was running away, and his part was running after me until he caught me."[52]

The doctrine of Irresistible Grace affirms that the salvation of the elect comes about not because man does his part, but because God does his part. The Lord quickens his elect and brings them to spiritual life from spiritual death. He pursues them and overwhelms all obstacles to bring them to himself.

---

[52] See Boice and Ryken, *The Doctrines of Grace*, 153–154.

Chapter 5
PERSEVERANCE OF THE SAINTS

The well-known chorus of Daniel Whittle's 1883 hymn repeats the text of 2 Timothy 1:12:

I know whom I have believed
And am persuaded that he is able
To keep that which I've committed
Unto him against that day.

The contemporary hymn "In Christ Alone" concludes with a similar sentiment by alluding to John 10:29:

No power of hell, no scheme of man,
Can ever pluck me from his hand:
Till He returns or calls me home,
Here in the power of Christ I'll stand.

The doctrine both these songs extol is that of the final and definite perseverance of the saints. This teaching is the fifth and final link in the chain of the doctrines of grace.

The doctrine of the perseverance of the saints maintains that the Lord is not only responsible for the plan, accomplishment, and application of redemption but also that he preserves or keeps believers in the faith. Some prefer to call this doctrine "the *preservation* of the saints." This doctrine affirms that God is true to his word and keeps his promises to the saints. As Paul reminds us, "scripture saith, Whosoever believeth on him shall not be ashamed" (Rom. 10:11, citing Isa. 28:16). Southern Presbyterian theologian Robert Lewis Dabney stated, "there is no room, without unfaithfulness in the Father, for the final falling away of a single star out of our Savior's purchased crown."[53]

This doctrine holds that if any person is truly saved, though he may backslide for a season and grieve the Spirit, he will not ultimately fall away from the state of grace. The Gospels provide a perfect example of the difference between the saint who stumbles to rise again and the apostate who sinks lower never to rise in the contrast between Peter (a believer who backslid and was restored) and Judas (a false professor who apostatized).

We find a classic statement of this doctrine in the opening paragraph of Chapter 17 ("Of the Perseverance of the Saints") in the Second London [Baptist] Confession. It reads in part:

> Those whom God hath accepted in the beloved, effectually called and sanctified by his Spirit, and given the precious faith of his elect unto, can neither totally nor finally fall from the state of grace, but shall certainly persevere therein to the end, and be eternally saved, seeing the gifts and callings of God are without repentance, whence he still begets and nourishes in them faith, repentance, love, joy hope, and all the graces of the Spirit unto immortality; and though many storms and floods arise and beat against them, yet they shall never be able

---

[53] Robert L. Dabney, *The Five Points of Calvinism* (1871; repr., Harrisonburg, VA: Sprinkle Publications, 1992), 71.

to take them off that foundation and rock which by faith they are fastened upon; notwithstanding, through unbelief and the temptations of Satan, the sensible sight of the light and love of God may for a time be clouded and obscured from them, yet he is still the same, and they shall be surely kept by the power of God unto salvation, where they shall enjoy their purchased possession, they being engraven upon the palm of his hands, and their names having been written in the book of life from all eternity. (2LCF 17.1)

This doctrine contends that if you are truly saved, you cannot become unsaved. God himself keeps you saved. Just as in creation God continues to keep the world in operation, "upholding all things by the word of his power" (Heb 1:3), so, when he makes a spiritual new creation, he keeps that person alive in Christ.

Observations on the Doctrine of the Perseverance of the Saints

(1) The Perseverance of the Saints rests on firm biblical foundations.

This doctrine has its biblical roots in the covenant relationship between the God of the Old Testament and the people of Israel. Despite Israel's repeated covenant violations and the corresponding just chastening they receive from the Lord, God's people are never completely abandoned. This relationship is perhaps best captured in the book of Hosea as the prophet remains a faithful husband to Gomer, despite her many infidelities, in a symbolic union that pictures the Lord's faithfulness to unfaithful Israel. At the close of the book of Hosea, the Lord says of Israel: "I will heal their backsliding, I will love them freely: for mine anger is turned away from him" (14:4). The Lord declares that he will not abandon Israel but will keep her.

In the New Testament, the Lord Jesus himself teaches this great doctrine, with respect to his relationship with his disciples. He speaks clearly of his unending love for those who are his own. In John 6:37 Christ says, "and him that cometh to me I will in no wise cast out." He then adds, "And this is the Father's will which hath sent me, that of all which he giveth me I should lose nothing, but should raise it up again at the last day" (6:39). To reject this doctrine would be to reject Christ's declaration that he will lose "nothing" (no one) who is his own. There is, indeed, great security for the believer, who is held firmly in the Lord's hand: "And I give unto them eternal life; and they shall never perish, neither shall any man pluck them out of my hand. My Father, which gave them me, is greater than all; and no man is able to pluck them out of my Father's hand" (John 10:28–29).

This doctrine was then heralded by the apostles. In his epistle to the church at Philippi, the apostle Paul affirms that the God of Scripture is faithful to finish what he has started in the lives of believers and in the church: "Being confident of this very thing, that he which hath begun a good work in you will perform it until the day of Jesus Christ" (Phil. 1:6). Peter, likewise, affirms that God himself is the one who adds the preservatives that keep the Christian in the faith. In his first epistle, Peter refers to the "Elect" as those "who are kept by the power of God through faith unto salvation ready to be revealed in the last time" (1 Pet. 1:2, 5).

Perhaps the grandest statement of this doctrine comes from Paul in Romans 8:33–39 when he asks, "Who shall lay any thing to the charge of God's elect?" (8:33) and "Who shall separate us from the love of Christ? shall tribulation, or distress, or persecution, or famine, or nakedness, or peril, or sword?" (8:35). Paul responds, "Nay, in all these things we are more than conquerors through him that loved us. For I am persuaded, that neither death, nor life, nor angels, nor principalities, nor powers nor things present, nor things to come, nor height, nor depth nor any other creature, shall be able to separate us from the love of God, which is in Christ Jesus our Lord" (8:37–39).

(2) THE PERSEVERANCE OF THE SAINTS IS A BETTER DESCRIPTION THAN "ONCE SAVED, ALWAYS SAVED" OR "ETERNAL SECURITY."

"Once saved, always saved" and "eternal security" are terms that are sometimes used in evangelical Christian circles. It is sometimes implied that these terms are equivalent to the doctrine of the Perseverance of the Saints. In fact, these terms run the risk of introducing a deformity of the doctrine. Subtly implied in these terms is the notion that once one professes faith in Christ it makes no difference how he lives from that point forward. This view is sometimes linked with the theology of the "carnal Christian" as opposed to the "spiritual Christian," based, in part, on a misreading of Paul's use of the terms "carnal" and "spiritual" in 1 Corinthians 3:1–4. Some even speak of the possibility of Jesus being a man's "Savior" but not his "Lord."

The biblical doctrine of perseverance, however, is related not only to the doctrine of salvation but also to sanctification. A verbal profession of faith alone is not conclusive evidence that one has been genuinely converted. Christ himself taught: "Not everyone that saith unto me, Lord, Lord, shall enter into the kingdom of heaven; but he that doeth the will of my Father, which is in heaven" (Matt. 7:21). The doctrine of the Perseverance of the Saints is more robust than the concepts of "once saved, always saved" or "eternal security" and should be preferred to it.

(3) THE PERSEVERANCE OF THE SAINTS DOES NOT IMPLY PERFECT HOLINESS IN THIS LIFE.

Though kept in a state of salvation and, at least to some degree, in a state of practical holiness, this doctrine does not imply that believers might ever reach a state of complete perfection on this side of the kingdom. One might well speak of the believer immediately attaining a status of "definitive sanctification" when he is saved. He joins the circle of the "saints" (the "holy ones") of God. He has the hope of the final resurrection and the promise of the final state of glorification (Rom. 8:30). In this life, however, he only begins the process of progressive sanctification.

The apostle Paul could write about his own life, striving for knowledge of Christ: "Not as though I had already attained, either were already perfect: but I follow after, if that I may apprehend that for which also I am apprehended of Christ Jesus" (Phil. 3:12). To this he adds, "Brethren, I count not myself to have apprehended . . . I press toward the mark for the prize of the high calling of God in Christ Jesus" (Phil. 3:13–14). The apostle John likewise warns, "If we say that we have no sin, we deceive ourselves, and the truth is not in us" (1 John 1:8). The various biblical calls to holiness within the New Testament itself are, in fact, evidence that believers need constantly to strive toward holy living (e.g., "Flee fornication" [1 Cor. 6:18]; "flee from idolatry" [1 Cor. 10:14]; "Flee also youthful lusts" [2 Tim. 2:22]); "be ye holy in all manner of conversation" [1 Pet. 1:15]; "keep yourselves from idols" [1 John 5:21]). If we were already perfectly holy, such exhortations would be unnecessary.

(4) OBJECTION PASSAGES TO THE PERSEVERANCE OF THE SAINTS DO NOT ACTUALLY REFER TO SAINTS FALLING AWAY.

Those who reject this doctrine sometimes appeal to passages of Scripture that they claim offer a contradiction to it. Close and careful inspection, however, reveals that these "objection" passages do not refer to the saved falling away. Instead, these involve either (1) descriptions of false professors of the faith; or (2) are warnings that are part of the very means of keeping the saints secure in their faith.

First, Scripture indicates that there will be false professors. We have already mentioned the example of Judas from among the Twelve, whom Christ refers to as the "son of perdition" saying "those that thou gavest me I have kept, and none of them is lost, but the son of perdition" (John 17:12). Paul also mentions Hymenaeus and Alexander who "concerning faith have made shipwreck" and had to be "delivered unto Satan, that they may learn not to blaspheme" (1 Tim. 1:19-20). In Paul's letters we also read of Demas who forsook Christ, because he "loved this present world" (2 Tim. 4:10; cf. Col. 4:14; Philem. 1:24).

The roots of this instruction, however, can be traced to the teaching ministry of Christ himself. In his Parable of the Sower, the Lord Jesus speaks of the seed that falls on the "stony ground" and the "thorny ground", which only appears to make a start, but which ultimately fails (cf. Matt. 13:1-9, 18-23; Mark 4:1-9, 13-20; Luke 8:4-8, 11-18). In Hebrews, likewise, we find a description of those who taste the heavenly gift but who fall away and so prove to be bad soil. The inspired author gives warnings against those who "were once enlightened, and have tasted the heavenly gift, and were made partakers of the Holy Ghost" (Heb. 6:4), noting that if they fall away, it is impossible "to renew them again unto repentance; seeing they crucify to themselves the Son of God afresh, and put him to an open shame" (Heb. 6:6). They prove to be barren soil: "But that which beareth thorns and briars is rejected, and is nigh unto cursing; whose end is to be burned" (Heb 6:8). The apostle John, likewise, in his first epistle also speaks of those who "went out from us, but they were not of us" (1 John 2:19). False professors are to be expected. And when a false professor does not continue in the faith, this does not contradict the doctrine of the Perseverance of the Saints.

Second, Scripture contains constant providential warnings for the believer against the dangers of falling away. This continues the theme we saw in Hebrews 6. It is also found in frequent challenges for the believer to be constantly examining his spiritual state. Here are a few such challenges:

> Wherefore let him that thinketh he standeth take heed lest he fall. (1 Cor. 10:12)

> Examine yourselves, whether ye be in the faith; prove your own selves. Know ye not your own selves, how that Jesus Christ is in you, except ye be reprobates? (2 Cor. 13:5)

> Wherefore the rather, brethren, give diligence to make your calling and election sure: for if ye do these things, ye shall never fall (2 Pet. 1:10)

Such warnings do not negate the promises described earlier. The Scripture cannot be broken (John 10:35), and one part of it does not stand in contradiction with another. No one can snatch the believer out of the Father's hand (John 10:29). These warning and challenging passages are, in fact, part of the very means God has provided to spur and provoke the believer on toward perseverance in the faith!

The nineteenth-century Presbyterian theologian R. L. Dabney offers the following parable to help us understand Scriptural warnings to the saints about backsliding:

> I watch a wise, intelligent, watchful, and loving mother, who is busy about her household work. There is a bright little girl

playing about the room, the mother's darling. I hear her say, "take care, baby dear, don't go near that bright fire, for you might get burned."

Do I argue thus? Hear that woman's words! I infer from them that the woman's mind is made up to let that darling child burn itself to death unless its own watchfulness shall suffice to keep it away from the fire, the caution of an ignorant, impulsive, fickle little child. What a heartless mother!

But I do not infer thus! I know that this mother knows the child is a rational creature, and that rational cautions are one specific means for keeping it at a safe distance from the fire; therefore she does right to address such cautions to the child; she would not speak thus if she thought it were a mere kitten or puppy dog, and would rely on nothing short of tying it by the neck to the table leg. But I also know that the watchful mother's mind is fully made up that the darling child shall not burn itself at this fire. If the little one's impulsiveness and short memory cause it to neglect the maternal cautions, I know that I shall see that good woman instantly drop her instruments of labor and draw back her child with physical force from that fire, and then most rationally renew her cautions to the child as a most reasonable agent with more emphasis. And if the little one proves still heedless and willful, I shall see her again rescued by physical force, and at last I shall see the mother impressing her cautions on the child's mind more effectually, perhaps by passionate caresses, or perhaps by a good switching, both alike the expression of faithful love.[54]

---

[54] Dabney, *The Five Points of Calvinism*, 78–79.

Can we imagine that our loving heavenly Father is less diligent and caring in his oversight of his children than the mother in Dabney's illustration?

Conclusion

Something must also be said at this point regarding the relationship of the doctrine of the Perseverance of the Saints with the other doctrines of grace. Some would claim to reject one, several, or even all of the other points and still maintain a belief in the perseverance of the saints. Such a position is logically inconsistent, however, since, as already noted, all five points must be understood as hanging together. The believer remains a believer, because while he was a spiritually dead sinner (in a state of depravity) God chose him in Christ before the foundation of the world (election); Christ died for his sins on the cross (particular redemption); and God sovereignly drew him to himself (irresistible grace).

The true Arminian is, at the least, logically consistent. He not only makes salvation dependent on the free will choice of man, but he makes remaining in the faith dependent on man's free will as well. Those—like Free Will Baptists, Methodists, and Nazarenes— who reject the other doctrines of grace wholesale—total depravity, unconditional election, limited atonement, and irresistible grace—also logically reject the perseverance of the saints. Hybrid views necessarily run into logical inconsistencies.

If it is somehow morally wrong for God to extend irresistible grace to overcome spiritual deadness and secure salvation, would it not be equally wrong for God to keep someone in the faith "against his will"? To be completely consistent, this would also introduce the unseemly notion that even in heaven, in the glorified state, one might be able to apostatize and be sent to hell. The converse would also be possible. One could be in hell and then freely choose to be in heaven. Even full Arminians are often inconsistent here, as they reject these scenarios, yet somehow hold that the standards exercised in this life are changed in the life to come. How much more pleasing it is to hold with firmness to the doctrines of grace and to see how the doctrine of divine preservation consistently fits not only with logical order but, most importantly, with biblical revelation.

Charles Spurgeon offered this practical, spiritual endorsement for this doctrine:

> I do not know how some people, who believe that a Christian can fall from grace, manage to be happy. It must be a very commendable thing in them to be able to get through a day without despair. If I did not believe the doctrine of the final perseverance of the saints, I think I should be of all men the most miserable, because I should lack any ground of comfort. I could not say, whatever state of heart I came into, that I should be like a well-spring of water, whose stream fails not; I should rather have to take the comparison of an intermittent spring, that might stop of a sudden, or a reservoir, which I had not reason to expect would always be full. I believe that the happiest of Christians and the truest of Christians are those who never dare to doubt God, but who take His Word simply as it stands, and believe it, and ask no questions, just feeling assured that if God has said it, it will be so. . . .[55]

---

[55] C. H. Spurgeon. *Autobiography*, vol. 1, *The Early Years*, (1897; repr., Edinburgh/Carlisle, PA: Banner of Truth, 1962), 169–170.

Spurgeon added:

> There is no living soul who holds more firmly to the doctrines of grace than I do, and if any man asks me whether I am ashamed to be called a Calvinist, I answer—I wish to be called nothing but a Christian; but if you ask me, do I hold the doctrinal views which were held by John Calvin, I reply, I do in the main hold them, and rejoice to avow it.[56]

Finally, Spurgeon said of these doctrinal convictions: "It is a nickname to call it Calvinism; Calvinism is the gospel, and nothing else."[57] Indeed, the doctrines of God's free grace—including the doctrine of final perseverance—are at the core of the good news.

[56] Spurgeon, *Autobiography*, 173.
[57] Spurgeon, *Autobiography*, 168.

Bibliography

The Baptist Confession of Faith & The Baptist Catechism. Birmingham, AL: Solid Ground Christian Books, 2010.

The Heidelberg Catechism. Grand Rapids, MI: Reformation Heritage Books, 2016.

Baxter, Richard. *The Reformed Pastor*. 1656. Edited by William Brown. 1892. Edinburgh/Carlisle, PA: Banner of Truth, 1989.

Beeke, Joel R.. *The Heritage Reformed Congregations: Who We Are and What We Believe*. Grand Rapids, MI: Reformation Heritage Books, 2007.

Biema, David Van. "Ten Ideas Changing the World Right Now." In *Time Magazine* 173, no. 12 (March 23, 2009). https://content.time.com/time/specials/packages/article/0,28804,1884779_1884782_1884760,00.html

Bingham, Matthew C., Chris Caughey, R. Scott Clark, Crawford Gribben, and D. G. Hart. *On Being Reformed: Debates Over a Theological Identity*. Cham, Switzerland: Palgrave Pivot, 2018.

Boice, James Montgomery and Philip Graham Ryken. *The Doctrines of Grace*. Wheaton, IL: Crossway, 2002.

Bunyan, John. *The Holy War*. 1682. Reprinted, Grand Rapids, MI: Baker Books, 1978.

Calvin, John. *Calvin's Commentaries*. Calvin Translation Society. 22 vols. Grand Rapids, MI: Baker Books, 2009.

———. *Institutes of the Christian Religion*. Vol. 1, edited by John T. McNeil. Louisville: Westminster John Knox Press, 1960.

Chantry, Walter. *Today's Gospel: Authentic or Synthetic?* Edinburgh/Carlisle, PA: Banner of Truth, 1970.

Clark, R. Scott. *Recovering the Reformed Confession: Our Theology, Piety, and Practice*. Philipsburg, NJ: P&R, 2008.

Collins, Hercules. *An Orthodox Catechism*. Edited by Michael A. G. Haykin and G. Stephen Weaver, Jr.. Palmdale, California: RBAP, 2014.

Dabney, Robert L.. *The Five Points of Calvinism.* 1871. Harrisonburg, VA: Sprinkle Publications, 1992.

———. "The System of Alexander Campbell: An Examination of Its Leading Points". In *Dabney's Discussions*, vol. 1, 314–49. Harrisonburg, VA: Sprinkle Publications, 1992. First published in *Southern Presbyterian Review* July, 1880.

Duncan, J. Ligon. "The Resurgence of Calvinism in America." In *Calvin for Today*, edited by Joel R. Beeke, 227–240. Grand Rapids, MI: Reformation Heritage, 2009.

Fischer, Austin. *Young, Restless, No Longer Reformed: Black Holes, Love, and a Journey In and Out of Calvinism.* Eugene, OR: Cascade Books, 2014.

Fuller, Andrew. "Creeds and Subscriptions." In *The Complete Works of the Rev. Andrew Fuller,* vol. 3, 449–451. Harrisonburg, VA: Sprinkle Publications, 1988.

Hansen, Colin. *Young, Restless, Reformed: A Journalist's Journey with the Young Calvinists.* Wheaton, IL: Crossway, 2008.

Hatch, Nathan O.. *The Democratization of American Christianity.* New Haven, CT: Yale University Press, 1989.

Helm, Paul. *Calvin and The Calvinists.* Edinburgh/Carlisle, PA: The Banner of Truth, 1982.

Kendall R. T.. *Calvin and English Calvinism to 1649.* Oxford: Oxford University Press, 1981.

Lloyd-Jones, D. Martyn. *Spiritual Depression: Its Causes and Cure.* Grand Rapids, MI: Eerdmans, 1965.

Lumpkin, William L.. *Baptist Confessions of Faith.* Valley Forge, PA: Judson Press, 1969.

Luther, Martin. *The Bondage of the Will.* Translated by J. I. Packer and O. R. Johnson. London: James Clarke, 1957.

McBeth, H. Leon. *The Baptist Heritage.* Nashville, TN: B&H, 1987.

Meadows, D. Scott. *God's Astounding Grace: The Doctrines of Grace Simply Explained from Scripture for Berean Christians.* North Bergen, NJ: Pillar and Ground, 2012.

Murray, Iain H.. *Wesley and Men Who Followed.* Edinburgh/Carlisle, PA: Banner of Truth Trust, 2003.

Murray, John. *Redemption Accomplished and Applied.* Grand Rapids, MI: Eerdmans, 1955.

——. *The Epistle to the Romans.* New International Commentary on the New Testament. Grand Rapids, MI: Eerdmans, 1968, 1997.

Owen, John. *The Death of Death in the Death of Christ.* Edinburgh/Carlisle, PA: Banner of Truth, 1959.

Packer, J. I.. *Evangelism and the Sovereignty of God.* Downers Grove, IL: IVP, 1961.

Palmer, Edwin H.. *The Five Points of Calvinism.* Enlarged ed.. Grand Rapids, MI: Baker Books, 1980.

Peterson, Robert A. and Michael D. Williams. *Why I Am Not an Arminian.* Downers Grove, IL: InterVarsity Press, 2004.

Poh, Boon-Sing. *The Fundamental of our Faith: Studies on the 1689 Baptist Confession of Faith.* Damansara Utama, Malaysia: Good News Enterprise, 2017.

Poole, Matthew. *A Commentary on the Holy Bible*. Vol. 3. Peabody, MA: Hendrickson, 2010.

Renihan, James M.. *Edification and Beauty: The Practical Ecclesiology of the English Particular Baptists, 1675–1705*. Milton Keynes, UK: Paternoster Press, 2008.

———. *To the Judicious and Impartial Reader: An Exposition of the 1689 London Baptist Confession of Faith*. Cape Coral, Florida: Founders Ministries, 2022.

Published in the UK as *Confessing the Faith*. Vol 2. *The Second London Baptist Confession of Faith*. Macclesfield, UK: Broken Wharfe, 2022.

Riddle, Jeffrey T.. "Review: Young, Restless, No Longer Reformed." In *Puritan Reformed Journal* 7, no. 2 (July 2015): 277–279.

Schaff, Philip. *The Creeds of Christendom*. Vol. 3. Grand Rapids, MI: Baker Books, 1998.

Spencer, Duane Edward. *TULIP: The Five Points of Calvinism in the Light of Scripture*. Grand Rapids, MI: Baker Books, 1979.

Spurgeon, C. H.. *Autobiography*. 2 vols. 1897–1900. Reprinted, Edinburgh/Carlisle, PA: Banner of Truth, 1973.

Venning, Ralph. *The Sinfulness of Sin*. 1669. Reprinted, Edinburgh/Carlisle, PA: Banner of Truth, 1993.

Waldron, Samuel E. *A Modern Exposition of the 1689 Baptist Confession of Faith*. 5th ed. Darlington: Evangelical Press, 2016

———. *Baptist Roots in America*. Boonton, NJ: Simpson, 1991.

Walker, Jeremy. *New Calvinism Considered: A Personal and Pastoral Assessment*. Darlington: Evangelical Press, 2013.

Walls, Jerry L. and Joseph R. Dongell. *Why I Am Not a Calvinist*. Downers Grove, IL: InterVarsity Press, 2004.